NAVIGATING YOUR RIGHTS

The Utah Legal Guide for
Those 55 and Over

NAVIGATING YOUR RIGHTS

The Utah Legal Guide for Those 55 and Over

By Jilenne Gunther

Foreword by Olene S. Walker, former Governor of Utah

Distributed by:
Utah Department of Human Services
Division of Aging and Adult Services
195 North 1950 West
Salt Lake City, Utah 84116

Published 2011 by State of Utah

First Edition

Publisher's Cataloging-in-Publication Data

Gunther, Jilenne

Navigating Your Rights: The Utah Legal Guide for Those 55 and Over.

Jilenne Gunther; foreword by former Governor Olene S. Walker.

First Edition

p. cm.

Includes index.

ISBN: 978-0-615-50787-3

1. Law 2. Aging 3. Utah 4. Legal Assistance to Older People 5. End-of-life Care 6. Grandparents' Rights 7. Elder Abuse 8. Consumer Rights 9. Estate Planning 10. Housing for Older People 11. Legal Resources 12. Death 13. Government Benefits

Copy Editing: Tressa Hiddenfriend and Elisabeth Guyon

Editing: Dan Hogan and Jane Clayson

Cover Design: RIESTER Advertising

Layout Design: David Stevens

Printed in the United States of America

To my favorite 55 year old — my mom

FOREWORD

By Olene S. Walker
Former Governor of Utah

You are holding in your hands the only book specifically designed to help Utahns over the age of 55 that explains legal issues. With help from the baby boomers, the 55-plus population is the fastest-growing segment in the state.

As one of the 503,694 Utahns in this age group and as former Governor, I am constantly faced with legal decisions. As we age, we have more concerns about laws related to retirement, end-of-life issues, advance directives, estate planning, health care, long-term care planning, and consumer fraud, among others. Some of the most common questions need simple answers. When do I start receiving Social Security? Is a will created with computer software valid? How do I avoid probate? Can I deed my house to my kids now?

Navigating the law regarding aging issues and questions can be challenging. Where do you go to find information and answers? There are many laws, and they are not written in plain English.

Yet these laws affect us. They affect our health, our finances, and our social needs. To avoid the pitfalls of making ill-informed decisions, it is essential that we empower ourselves through education in this aging game.

The goal of this book is to educate older Utahns about various law and aging issues. The end result is the hope that more Utahns will be comfortable with the law and make informed legal decisions.

This book was developed because 60% of older Utahns surveyed said they wanted a legal guidebook more than any other service or program. Since that time, Jilenne Gunther, with the support of The Borchard Foundation Center on Law and Aging and the Utah Division of Aging and Adult Services, has been working tirelessly with attorneys and aging experts to respond to that request. This book is the result. It makes the law simple to understand and navigate. It is written in plain language and an easy-to-read format. At the end of each chapter there is a listing of agencies and organizations to contact for more information. Throughout the book you will see symbols for important things, warnings, and times when you need to hire an attorney. I want to thank Jilenne Gunther for her great contribution in helping senior citizens understand Utah law.

Olene S. Walker
Former Governor of Utah

CONTENTS

Chapter 1
PROTECTING YOURSELF FROM SCAMS AND SALES . .1

Scams .2

Identity Theft 5

Junk Mail 9

Telemarketers 9

Door-to-Door Salesmen 11

Contractors 12

Reverse Mortgages 13

More Information 16

Chapter 2
KNOWING YOUR CONSUMER RIGHTS 19

Complaints 20

Demand Letter. 21

Contracts 23

Utilities 24

Debt Collection 26

Bankrupcty 27

More Information 29

Chapter 3
PREVENTING AND PROTECTING YOURSELF FROM ABUSE. 31

Victims and Their Abusers 32

Signs of Abuse 33

Financial Exploitation 34

Reporting Abuse. 37

More Information 38

Chapter 4

CARING FOR GRANDCHILDREN 39

Caring for Grandchildren 40

Delegation of Parental Powers 40

School Enrollment 42

Visitation Rights 42

Kinship Care 44

Guardianship 45

Adoption 47

More Information 48

Chapter 5

LEARNING ABOUT BENEFITS 49

Social Security 50

Social Security Retirement 51

Social Security Family Benefits 53

Social Security Disability 54

Supplemental Security Income 55

Applying for Social Security 56

Appealing Social Security 58

Veteran Benefits 59

Pensions 62

More Information 64

Chapter 6

OBTAINING MEDICAL INSURANCE 65

Medicare 66

Medicare Benefits 67

Applying for Medicare 76

Appealing Medicare 77

Other Medical Insurance 82

Medicaid 83

Medigap 84

Long-Term Care 84

Counseling. 87

More Information 88

Chapter 7

FINDING HOUSING OPTIONS. 89

Options and Assessments 90

Living in Your Home 92

Independent Living 97

Higher Levels of Care 99

More Information 106

Chapter 8

ORGANIZING YOUR ASSETS: ESTATE PLANNING 107

Wills 108

Probate. 111

Trust 113

Updating Estate Planning 115

Taxes 116

Property 117

More Information 120

Chapter 9

KEEPING THE POWER: END-OF-LIFE PLANNING 121

Advance Health Care Directives 122

Guardianship 127

Power of Attorney 131

More Information 134

Chapter 10

MAKING ARRANGEMENTS: DEATH OF A LOVED ONE 135

Priority of Tasks 136

First Day. 136

First Week 138

First Month 139

More Information 144

Chapter 11

GETTING LEGAL HELP: WHERE TO GO FROM HERE

GETTING LEGAL HELP:
WHERE TO GO FROM HERE. 145

Solving the Problem Yourself. 146

Getting Brief Legal Help 147

Hiring an Attorney 149

More Information 151

GLOSSARY 153

APPENDIX A: GOVERNMENT AGENCIES 157

APPENDIX B: NONPROFIT AGENCIES 161

APPENDIX C: ACKNOWLEDGMENTS 163

INDEX 168

INTRODUCTION

"We already gave you the films," responded the nurse. This was an easy way of not being bothered. I had taken Kaye to every appointment, and I knew she had not received any pre or post-operative films, and she knew something had gone wrong during her eye surgery. Kaye was now a partially blind 70-year-old accompanied by myself, a naive 14-year-old. We walked home without the films.

This story is important to me because of the relationship I had with Kaye. I met her when I was 12 years old and she was in her sixties. I loved hearing her stories. During World War II, she had been a nurse in Malaysia. She fell in love with and married one of the men who was under her care. After the war they desperately wanted to return to his homeland, but the Iron Curtain prevented them from doing so. Instead, they moved to New York, where her husband was the Polish voice for Radio Free Europe. I gained a great respect for Kaye as I listened to the stories about her life and their struggles to bring freedom to those in her husband's homeland.

I watched a woman who had worked to bring freedom to others, now have that freedom taken away from her at the end of her life. Where would Kaye go today to resolve this problem? Where do you go today to get answers to legal questions? Like Kaye, many people have questions, as they approach 55: How do I apply for Medicare? How do I hire a contractor? How do I avoid today's scams?

If you are in this situation, this book is perfect for you. It will answer these questions and many more. And it's what you requested. In a survey, Utahns 60 and over said they wanted a legal resource guide more than several other services. Here it is.

In this book, I'll tell you how to navigate your rights, from asserting your rights as a grandparent to creating a health care power of attorney. I'll even explain when you should hire an attorney and when you can save your money.

This book is for anyone who has questions about elder law — caregivers, families, aging professionals, social workers, attorneys — but it was written especially with those 55 and over in mind. It's a reference guide written in question and answer format. You can pick it up and turn to any page and start reading. If you are looking for a particular subject, use either the table of contents at the front of the book or the index at the back.

Each chapter starts off with a roadmap that lays out what is in the chapter. Every chapter is broken into subsections relating to the chapter topic. For example, the chapter entitled "Protecting Yourself from Scams and Sales" is broken into seven sections — Scams, Identity Theft, Junk Mail, Telemarketers, Door-to-Door Salesmen, Contractors and Reverse Mortgages.

Throughout the book are icons that highlight important things--tips, dangers, and warnings about legal jargon.

 Important Things — This denotes important things. If you read anything, read the section by this icon.

 Good Tips — This denotes great tips to help prevent future problems.

 Warning to Proceed with Caution — This warning sign points out areas you should be cautious about.

 Need an Attorney — Let's face it, even I would rather spend my money on something other than an attorney. This icon highlights areas that will tell you whether or not you need an attorney.

 Legal Nerd Talk — I'm a big believer in using plain English, but sometimes specialized words just can't be avoided. So when you see this icon, take it as a warning or an apology that legal jargon is coming up.

You don't have to read the whole book at once. It's a need-to-know book. You can pick it up whenever you have a question. If you need to know how to get rid of junk mail — pick it up. If you need to know how to write a complaint — pick it up.

Almost no book can be a complete resource, so at the end of each chapter is a section entitled "More Information" that lists organizations that you can contact for additional information. Some organizations do not take phone calls; in these cases only a website address is provided. The book also includes a glossary and appendix with helpful legal resources.

With that, pick this book up whenever you need your questions answered.

DISCLAIMER

This book is intended to provide general legal information. It is not a full or exhaustive explanation of the legal topics in this book. You should not consider it the rendering of legal advice that is applicable to any particular situation. It is your responsibility to consult with competent legal counsel regarding any information discussed in this book. Nothing in this book should be used as a substitute for advice from legal counsel. If you need legal advice, you should obtain the services of an attorney.

This information is intended, but not guaranteed, to be accurate and current. Since laws can change rapidly, this information is provided without warranty or guarantee. The applicability of some laws discussed can vary based on jurisdiction and the interpretations of courts within each county.

The author and those who contributed content do not constitute a law firm and do not represent you as the reader. In no way will the author be liable to the reader or any other person or entity for damages arising from the reliance, use, inability to use, or lack of action based on this information. The author will not be responsible for any claims arising from errors, omissions, or inaccuracies in this book.

Chapter
1

PROTECTING YOURSELF FROM SCAMS AND SALES

In This Chapter, Learn:

- How to Avoid Scams
- How to Prevent Identity Theft
- What to do if You Are a Victim of Identity Theft
- How to Get Rid of Junk Mail
- How to Stop Telemarketers
- How to Get a Refund from a Door-to-Door Sale
- What to Know Before Hiring a Contractor
- Whether You Should Get a Reverse Mortgage
- About Much More

SCAMS

How do I avoid consumer scams?

- Don't give into high-pressure sales tactics.
- Take time to make decisions.
- Do your homework before hiring a contractor, giving to a charity, making an investment, or purchasing goods or services.
- Don't hire people that solicit your business.
- If it sounds too good to be true, it is!
- Ignore offers that go away if you don't act now.
- Ask for everything in writing, and don't sign until you understand and agree with the terms of the offer and consequences.
- Don't open your door to strangers and solicitors.

What are the top scams?

Medicare Scams

Watch out for Medicare con artists. Some con artists are trying to cash in on the Medicare program (see chapter 6). They call pretending to be Medicare employees offering health insurance programs. They ask you to sign up and pay over the phone. The catch is that they are not Medicare employees (because Medicare employees don't initiate calls to enroll you), they are not signing you up for a legitimate Medicare program, and any information you give them may be used to steal money and your identity.

Investments with "High Returns and Low Risks"

If you hear about an investment that is low risk with a high return, run away! If you want a high return, you have to take larger risks. Investigate carefully before purchasing an investment.

Travel Scams

"Free vacations" are not bargains. Free or bargain vacation deals often come with "hidden fees." For example, after accepting the vacation, you might be asked to pay a high tax or other fees. Or once you book the trip you may have to pay for upgrades so you can travel on the dates and to the destinations you desire. In the end, you have paid more for the "free" vacation than you initially expected.

Predatory Lending

Say no to predatory lending! Companies with predatory lending practices may target you with unfair and abusive loan terms through aggressive and deceptive sales tactics that take advantage of your lack of understanding. Predatory lending practices are commonly seen in situations where you have equity built up in your home and, faced with medical bills or home repairs, you decide to refinance. Predatory lending includes "loan flipping." This is when a lender convinces the homeowner to refinance several times. The lender entices you by promising cash or much lower mortgage payments. However, the refinancing may include an excessively high interest rate, unnecessary closing costs, or an undisclosed "balloon payment."

Living Trust Scams

Living trusts can be legitimate and a valuable estate planning tool. However, living trust scams are a growing concern as they are not appropriate for all people. Do your homework before getting a living trust. A trust is a person or organization that owns, holds, or manages your assets for the benefit of yourself or another. A living trust is when you create a trust while you are living. Property is moved into a trust, and the trustee (the person in charge of the trust) manages the property for the benefit of the beneficiaries.

Generally, people with lower incomes or small estates don't need a living trust. There are many false and misleading statements about the costs and benefits of living trusts. Some people may exaggerate the cost and length of probate, falsely imply AARP endorsement, tell you the court will force or could force you into a guardianship, or tell you that a living trust is the only way to protect yourself from probate and from the government taking your money. If you think you might need a living trust, talk to an estate planning attorney.

Foreclosure Rescue Scams

Run away from Rescue Scams! With the recent increase in the number of mortgage delinquencies and foreclosures, there has been an increase in the number of foreclosure rescue scams. These con artists create companies that advertise services to help you and others avoid foreclosure. However, they make misleading promises, take large fees, or fraudulently induce you into transferring the deed (a legal document that gives someone title to real property) of your home. In the end, you've received no help and are out of a home and out of money. For example, the con artist slips the deed into a stack of documents and you end up signing your deed over to the con artist. Alternatively, the con artist promises to save your home from foreclosure for a fee by negotiating with the bank or mortgage lender and rarely stops the foreclosure.

What to do if you have been scammed.

If you have been scammed, report it to the Federal Trade Commission (FTC) and the Utah Division of Consumer Protection (see the "More Information" section on page 16 for contact information).

IDENTITY THEFT

What is identity theft?

Some thieves want to steal your identity to profit from it. All they need is your name and Social Security Number to open an account and to buy goods or services in your name. This is a serious crime that can destroy your credit and cost you time and money.

Identity thieves will try anything to get your personal information. They will steal your wallet, go through your trash, and hack into your computer.

How do I prevent identity theft?

Be Very Cautious When Giving Out Personal Information

- Don't carry your Social Security card, passport, or birth certificate with you unless absolutely necessary.
- Very few people other than your employer, bank, Medicare, IRS, Medicaid, Motor Vehicle Department, brokerage, and the Social Security Administration (SSA) need your Social Security Number (SSN).
- If a company asks for your SSN, decline to provide it. Ask if you can give an alternative form of identification.

Be Careful about Your Trash

- Buy a shredder. Shred any paper that contains personal information, including receipts, bank statements, checks, and credit card offers.

Protect Your Computer

- Install anti-spyware and firewall software on your computer to prevent unauthorized access to your computer.

Scams and Sales

- Beware of any email that looks like it's from a legitimate company but states that your account has been compromised and you need to go to the link provided in the email. This is called phishing. The email is not from that company, but a scam. The link in the email takes you to a similar but fake website where you are asked to put in your personal information. Forward any phishing emails to the FTC at spam@uce.gov.

How will I know if my identity has been stolen?

 Warning Signs of Identity Theft Include:
- Your bills are late or don't arrive.
- Your mail is forwarded.
- You are denied credit for no reason.
- You receive bills for things you didn't purchase.

To detect identity theft you should review your financial statements and credit reports for discrepancies. Request a free copy of your credit report once a year from the Annual Credit Report Request Service or order a copy of your credit report from one of the major consumer credit reporting companies in the "More Information" section (page 16).

What should I do if I am a victim of identity theft?

If You Are a Victim of Identity Theft:

File a Police Report

This will prove to creditors that you are a victim of identity theft.

Contact a Major Consumer Credit Reporting Company

Ask that a fraud alert be placed on your credit report. This requires companies to call you before they extend credit under your name and SSN (see the "More Information" section on page 16 for contact information).

Close Tampered Accounts

Call the places where fraudulent accounts were tampered with or opened. Talk to someone in the fraud or security department. Ask them to close the account. Follow up with a written letter, and include supporting documents. Ask for a letter confirming that the account was closed and the debts were discharged.

File a Report and Complaint

File a complaint with the Federal Trade Commission. Also, file a report with the Utah Attorney General's Office (see the "More Information" section on page 17 for contact information).

JUNK MAIL

How do I get rid of junk mail?

Contact the Direct Marketing Association and request that your name be taken off mailing lists and that it not be sold or given to companies (see the "More Information" section on page 17). Don't fill out consumer and marketing surveys or sweepstakes entry forms.

TELEMARKETERS

How do I stop telemarketers from calling?

Hanging up only temporarily resolves the issue. There are better and more permanent ways to get telemarketers to stop calling. When the telemarketer calls, cut them off by saying, "We don't want to receive calls from your company. Put this number on your Do-Not-Call list."

Prevent Telemarketing Calls:

- Register with the Do-Not-Call Registry at 888-382-1222 or www.donotcall.gov.

- Don't fill out consumer and marketing surveys, warranty registration cards (you get warranty rights without the card), or sweepstakes entry forms.
- When doing business with companies, including charities, ask them to not "rent" or "sell" your number to any other organization.

What rules do telemarketers have to follow?

Telemarketers Cannot:

- Call before 8 a.m. or after 9 p.m.
- Call if your number is on the Do-Not-Call list (unless there is an exception).
- Deceive you to get you to sign up with the company.
- Fail to identify themselves.
- Block their telephone number from your caller identification service.
- Misrepresent their product or service.

If telemarketers violate these rules, you can file a complaint with the Utah Division of Consumer Protection (DCP), Federal Communications Commission (FCC), or the Federal Trade Commission (FTC). You can also file a lawsuit.

DOOR-TO-DOOR SALESMEN

How do I get my money back from a door-to-door salesman?

 The law protects you from door-to-door salesmen by giving you three business days to cancel the sale or the contract (a legal agreement between two or more parties). The rule applies if the salesman came to your home or to any place other than his place of business. However, this right to cancel does not cover purchases under $25.

To cancel the sale, send a written notice to the seller at the address listed on the contract. The notice must state that you don't want the goods or services. Mail the notice before midnight on the third business day. Send the notice by certified mail, with a return receipt request, and keep a copy for your records.

Generally, the salesman must give you back any payments you made within 30 days after the cancellation. You must return, within a reasonable time, any goods the salesman gave you.

CONTRACTORS

What should I know before hiring a contractor?

 Most of us at some time or another will hire a contractor to do a home repair or improvement. There are many contractors who do a great job, but there are some who do not. They may do substandard work, overcharge for "improvements," or not finish the job.

When Hiring a Contractor:

- Always get estimates for the job from two or three contractors who are recommended by friends or family.

- Speak to others who have hired the contractor. Ask about the quality, cost, and timeliness of the work.

- Check the Better Business Bureau (BBB) of Utah for complaints against the contractor. Make sure that the contractor has a business license and liability insurance by contacting the Utah Division of Occupational and Professional Licensing.

- Make sure that the contractor agrees to the following in writing: the price; a summary of the work to be done and materials to be used; start date and the estimated completion date; responsibility for clean up; guarantees; and financing and credit terms, if applicable.

- Agree in advance that full payment is not due until the work is complete.

What contractors should I avoid?

Avoid Contractors Who:

- Tell you the repair is urgent, when in reality it is not.

- Quote a price, then raise it because materials must be substituted.

- Don't give out their business address and only use a P.O. box.

- Come to your door seeking business.

- Ask for a deposit, especially a large deposit.

Can a contractor put a lien on my house?

If you fail to pay a contractor for labor, materials, or equipment, the contractor may file a mechanic's lien against your home. A mechanic's lien is a claim against your property for the cost of the contractor's work. If you don't pay the contractor, he or she can go to court and force the sale of your home. Once you have paid in full, the contractor must cancel or remove the mechanic's lien on your property.

REVERSE MORTGAGES

What is a reverse mortgage?

With a traditional mortgage, a lender finances the purchase of your home and you make monthly payments to the lender. To qualify, the lender checks your income to determine how much you can afford to pay back each month, and the amount you owe on the loan decreases with each monthly repayment to the lender.

With a "reverse" mortgage, you receive money from the lender and the loan is secured by your principal residence. Generally, there are no monthly repayments as long as you live in the home, and therefore, you do not need an income to qualify for a reverse mortgage. The amount you owe on the loan increases each time you receive money from the lender, and the interest is added to the outstanding loan balance. The loan is repaid when you sell your home, when you die, or when you no longer live there as your principal residence. If your home is sold and the lender is repaid, any money left over goes to you, your estate, or your heirs.

Why do people get a reverse mortgage?

A reverse mortgage can help a homeowner stay in their home and convert part of the equity in their home into cash. Many seniors use it to meet financial obligations, finance home repairs or improvements, pay health care expenses, and more.

What costs are involved in a reverse mortgage?

When Considering a Reverse Mortgage, Be Aware That:

• Lenders generally charge closing and other fees for a reverse mortgage.

- Your total debt increases over time as loan funds are given to you and the interest is charged on the balance.

- The reverse mortgage may have a fixed or adjustable rate. If it has an adjustable rate, it will likely change according to market conditions.

- Reverse mortgages use up some or all of the equity in your home, leaving fewer assets or no assets for you and your heirs.

- Because you retain title to your home, you still have to pay for property taxes, insurance, utilities, repairs, and other expenses.

- The interest on a reverse mortgage is not deductible on income tax returns until the loan is paid off in whole or part.

Should I get a reverse mortgage?

 A reverse mortgage should be a last resort option. For most people, their house is their largest asset. Keeping this financial safety net as long as possible is recommended.

So you should be cautious and research your options before talking to a lender about a reverse mortgage. If you are considering a reverse mortgage as a way to remain living in your present home, compare it to selling your home and using the proceeds to buy or rent a new home.

If someone tries to sell you something, such as an annuity, and suggests that a reverse mortgage is an easy way to pay for it, be skeptical. You should fully understand what you are buying and the cost of a reverse mortgage.

More Information

SCAMS

Report scams

Federal Trade Commission
877-FTC-HELP (382-4357)
www.ftc.gov

Utah Division of Consumer Protection
800-721-SAFE (721-7233)
801-530-6601
www.dcp.utah.gov

Information about scams

National Consumer Law Center
www.consumerlaw.org

National Fraud Information Center
www.fraud.org

IDENTITY THEFT

Check your credit report and report identity theft

Annual Credit Report Request Service
877-322-8228
www.annualcreditreport.com

Equifax
800-525-6285 (fraud alert)
800-685-1111 (credit reports)
www.equifax.com

Experian
888-397-3742 (fraud alert and credit reports)
www.experian.com

TransUnion
800-680-7289 (fraud alert)
800-916-8800 (credit reports)
www.transunion.com

Report identity theft

Utah Attorney General's Office, Identity Theft Reporting
www.idtheft.utah.gov

Federal Trade Commission's Identity Theft Hotline
877-IDTHEFT (438-4338)
www.ftc.gov/idtheft

TELEMARKETERS

Register your phone number on the National Do-Not-Call Registry

888-382-1222
www.donotcall.gov

File a complaint against a telemarketer

Utah Division of Consumer Protection
800-721-7233
801-530-6601
www.dcp.utah.gov

Federal Communications Commission
888-CALL-FCC (225-5322)
www.fcc.gov

Federal Trade Commission
877-FTC-HELP (382-4357)
www.ftc.gov

JUNK MAIL

Get your name removed from mailing lists by registering for the mail preference service

Direct Marketing Association
www.dmachoice.org

CONTRACTORS

Check complaints against contractors or file a complaint

Better Business Bureau of Utah
800-456-3907
801-892-6009
www.utah.bbb.org

Check contractor's business license and liability insurance or file a complaint

Utah Division of Occupational and Professional Licensing
866-275-3675
801-530-6628
www.dopl.utah.gov

Information about hiring a contractor

Federal Trade Commission
www.ftc.gov

National Association of Home Builders
www.nahb.org

REVERSE MORTGAGE

Information about reverse mortgages

AARP Foundation
888-687-2277
www.aarp.org

DOOR-TO-DOOR SALES

File a complaint regarding door-to-door sales

Utah Division of Consumer Protection
800-721-7233
801-530-6601
www.dcp.utah.gov

Chapter
2

KNOWING YOUR
CONSUMER RIGHTS

In This Chapter, Learn:

- How to Resolve a Complaint with a Business
- What to do Before Signing a Contract
- About Verbal Contracts
- How to Write a Simple Contract
- Your Utility Rights
- How to Dispute a Collection Debt
- The Basics of Bankruptcy
- About Much More

COMPLAINTS

How do I resolve a complaint with a business?

 So you have a problem with a business. Maybe it was a contractor who didn't do a good job, or a company that didn't give you your money back. If this happens you may try the following: call the business and try to work it out, write a demand letter, call the Better Business Bureau (BBB) and the Utah Division of Consumer Protection, and, in some cases, it may be appropriate for you to file a lawsuit.

Try Working It Out

- Your first approach should be to resolve this issue directly with the business.

Write a Demand Letter

- If you are unable to work out the issue, a demand letter states your complaint and explains how you want the company to resolve the issue.

File a Complaint with the Utah Better Business Bureau

- If you have a dispute with a company, you can file a complaint with the Utah Better Business Bureau. The BBB acts as a mediator between the consumer and the company.

File a Complaint with the Utah Division of Consumer Protection

- If you have questions about a specific transaction, you may contact the Utah Division of Consumer Protection. If it is determined that your complaint involves a matter that is handled by this Division, you can fill out the Complaint Form. (The Division handles telemarketing fraud, identity theft, and door-to-door sales, among many other types of consumer issues.) Send the complaint with relevant documents supporting your claim.

Utah Small Claims Court

- If your claim (the amount you are seeking) is $10,000 or under, you can file a lawsuit in Utah small claims court. You do not need an attorney to sue in small claims court.

DEMAND LETTER

How do I write a demand letter?

Use the Following Tips to Write a Good Demand Letter.

- Try to keep the letter to one page.
- Address the letter to the company's president.
- On the envelope write in bold "for immediate and personal attention."

- Provide a copy of the letter to the BBB and other consumer protection organizations, such as the Utah Division of Consumer Protection.

The letter should have four main parts.

Say Something Positive

- Start the letter by stating something positive about the company. For example, discuss how long you have been a satisfied customer.

State the Problem

- Be specific: include the date it occurred, what happened, and whom you spoke to in the company about the issue.

Tell Them What You Want

- State what you expect the company to do in return (for example, an apology, refund, exchange) and when you would like a response.

Include Your Contact Information

- Include your contact information so that the company can reply to your letter.

Contracts

What should I do before signing a contract?

- When buying, selling, or trading goods or services you enter into a contract. Many people never read the contract before signing it, which makes them unsure as to the agreed-upon legal and financial obligations.

- Before you sign a contract, stick to this important rule — read and understand every word in the contract.

- If you don't understand any part of the contract, ask questions or consult an attorney or knowledgeable friend.

- If you need more time, take a copy of the contract to review before you sign it.

- If there are blank spaces in the contract to be filled in later, don't sign the contract.

- If you and the other party agree on something that is not written in the document, add it to the contract. All parties must then initial the change.

- If you sign a contract, keep a copy.

What if I make a verbal contract?

People often make verbal contracts. You might loan a friend some money or sell a TV to a neighbor on a verbal agreement. While many verbal contracts are legally enforceable, they are very difficult to prove. It is wise to put any agreement in writing.

When should I have a written contract, and do I need an attorney for it?

 You should request a written contract whenever you make a major purchase, take out a loan, arrange for home repairs, or buy or sell real estate. If the contract is complex, you should ask an attorney to review it. Remember that it would be better and cost less to have an attorney review the contract before signing it than to have an attorney represent you in court afterwards because you signed a contract that you should not have signed.

How do I write a simple contract?

For small simple sales, such as the sale of a TV to a relative or neighbor, you should be able to draft a simple written contract yourself. There is no special language needed, but you should include the date and terms of the agreement and have all parties sign it.

UTILITIES

Can a utility company shut off my service?

If you don't pay your bill, the utility company can terminate your service. The

utility company must take the following steps before terminating your service*:

- Give you information on how you can avoid termination, such as how to set up a deferred payment plan, and how to request an extension based on a medical necessity.

- Notify you, a residential customer, in advance before shutting off your service: seven days for the phone utility companies and ten days for other utilities.

- Contact you by mail, telephone, or personal visit at least two days before terminating your service.

- During the winter months (October 1 to March 31), non-telephone utility companies must contact you by either telephone or a personal visit to your residence.

- Continue your services for a specified time period (usually no more than 30 days) if someone in your household is seriously ill and you provide a doctor's statement showing that shutting off services will aggravate the illness.

(*This does not apply to wireless phone service)

What if I have a dispute with a utility company?

The first thing you should do is contact the utility company to tell them you have a dispute. If the dispute is over a bill, you should continue to pay the non-disputed part of the bill.

If you are unable to resolve the dispute, you can file an informal complaint with the Utah Division of Public Utilities.

DEBT COLLECTION

What happens if I can't pay my bills?

If you are late in paying your bills, loan, or mortgage, your account might be sent to a collection agency. While you are obligated to pay your bills, the Fair Debt Collections Act regulates what a collection agent can and cannot do.

What can't debt collectors do?

Generally, Debt Collectors Cannot:

- Call you before 8 a.m. or after 9 p.m., harass you, or use profane language.
- Call you at work if they know your employer prohibits calls.
- Contact you after you have told them in writing to cease contact, except to tell you they are taking a specific action regarding the debt.
- Contact friends or inform others that you owe money.
- Threaten to take your property unless it is legal to do so.
- Threaten to file criminal charges or harm you.
- Collect your Social Security to pay your debt.

If I dispute the debt what should I do?

 Within five days of first contacting you, the collector must tell you the following in writing:

- How much you owe.
- The name of the creditor (whom you owe).
- What you can do if you dispute the charge.
- Unless you dispute the debt within 30 days, it will be assumed valid.
- If you dispute the debt, you must write to the collection agency within 30 days of receiving the first letter. To provide proof that you sent the letter send it by certified mail with return receipt requested. Upon receiving your letter, the collection agency will send you verification of the debt. The debt collector must stop contacting you until they send that verification.

BANKRUPCTY

What does it mean to file for bankruptcy?

When you file for bankruptcy you are stating that you don't have enough money to pay your bills and outstanding loans. Bankruptcy, when used properly, is a way to start a clean slate, reduce your debt, or develop a debt repayment plan.

Consumer Rights

Is filing for bankruptcy a good idea?

Bankruptcy should only be considered when you are in dire need. You need to consider the burden you cause to others when you are unable to pay your financial commitments. Also, bankruptcy affects your credit for up to 10 years. It will be difficult to obtain credit, a loan, or a mortgage. If you are able to get a loan, it may be at a higher interest rate.

Are there alternatives to filing for bankruptcy?

One alternative to bankruptcy is to negotiate a debt repayment plan or loan modification with your creditors.

What are the types of personal bankruptcy?

There are two common types of consumer bankruptcy — chapter 7 and chapter 13 under the Bankruptcy law. Whether you file a chapter 7 or chapter 13 case will depend on your situation, your income, and what kind of debt you have.

In a chapter 7 case, a bankruptcy trustee will sell your non-exempt unprotected property (e.g., stocks, bonds), if any, and distribute the money to your creditors. In a chapter 13 case, you ask the court to approve a debt repayment plan, where you pay all or a portion of your debts over three to five years.

Can I file for bankruptcy without an attorney?

While an individual can file for bankruptcy without an attorney, the new bankruptcy laws are complicated. Missing an important deadline or filing can affect your rights. Hiring an attorney is recommended.

More Information

COMPLAINTS

File a complaint against a company

Utah Division of Consumer Protection
800-721-7233
801-530-6601
www.dcp.utah.gov

Better Business Bureau of Utah
800-456-3907
801-892-6009
www.utah.bbb.org

Federal Trade Commission
877-FTC-HELP (382-4357)
www.ftc.gov

SMALL CLAIMS COURT

Information on filing a small claims suit

Utah State Courts' Self-Help Resource Center
www.utcourts.gov

UTILITIES

File a complaint against a utility company

Utah Division of Public Utilities
PO Box 146751
Salt Lake City, UT 84114-6751
800-874-0904
801-530-7622 (SLC)
www.publicutilities.utah.gov

BANKRUPTCY

Information on bankruptcy, such as how and whether you should file

Utah Legal Services
800-662-4245
801-328-8891
www.uls.state.ut.us

Utah State Courts' Self-Help Resource Center
www.utcourts.gov

American Bankruptcy Institute
www.abiworld.org

Chapter
3

PREVENTING AND PROTECTING YOURSELF FROM ABUSE

In This Chapter, Learn:

- Who the Victims and Abusers Are
- Why Abusers Don't Report Abuse
- About the Signs of Abuse
- How to Protect Yourself from Financial Exploitation
- How to Report Abuse
- About Much More

VICTIMS AND THEIR ABUSERS

Who are the victims and their abusers?

Abusers can be from all walks of life — friends, acquaintances, family members, or strangers. Abusers try to isolate and manipulate their victims so the victim will not tell someone about the abuse. They do this by preventing the victim from seeing friends, family members, and others. They also manipulate the victim into not trusting friends, while the abuser continues to gain the victim's trust.

Why don't victims report abuse?

Perhaps you know someone who has been abused, or perhaps you have been a victim yourself and you have never told anyone about that abuse. There are many reasons victims fear reporting abuse, including the fear that:

- No one will help.
- The abuser will retaliate.
- The relationship with the abuser will be lost, and the victim is dependent on the abuser.
- The abuser will get into trouble.
- Others will discover they have been abused.

SIGNS OF ABUSE

What are the signs of physical abuse?

Physical abuse occurs when a person is hurt in a way that causes injury or will likely cause injury. Signs of physical abuse include the following:

- Unexplained bruises, fractures, or welts.
- Sprains, injuries, or open wounds.
- Abrasions and lacerations.

What are the signs of emotional abuse?

Emotional abuse is the infliction of mental anguish or emotional distress. This occurs when a person is subjected to behavior such as yelling, swearing, ridiculing, harassing, or coercing. Signs of emotional abuse include the following:

- Low self-esteem.
- Emotional outbursts.
- Withdrawn attitude.

What are the signs of neglect?

Neglect occurs when a person does not have basic necessities like food, water, clothing, shelter, medical care, and personal care. This can occur through a senior's own neglect or a caretaker's neglect. Signs of neglect include the following:

- Lack of food, necessary medication, or medical care.

- Weight loss, dehydration, or malnutrition.
- Filthy living conditions.
- Poor hygiene.

What are the signs of financial exploitation?

Financial exploitation occurs when a person is deprived of their assets (things that a person owns that have value). Signs of financial exploitation include:

- Disappearance of possessions or money.
- Sudden withdrawals or transfers of funds to another person.
- Inability to afford food, clothes, or social activities.
- Money spent on items that the senior does not need.
- Changing a name on a deed may be cause for a concern (see below).
- Because financial abuse is so prevalent, the following section provides warning signs and helpful tips on how to protect yourself.

FINANCIAL EXPLOITATION

Who is doing the financial exploitation?

 The most important thing is to be careful about everyone, including family members. Most people don't believe financial exploitation can happen within their own family, but three out of four perpetrators are family members.

How can I protect myself from financial exploitation?

Ask for Help from Someone You Trust

Financial matters can be confusing and difficult. If you have questions or need assistance, ask for help from a trusted family member, friend, clergy, or other professional.

Stay Socially Active

Social isolation increases your risk of becoming a victim of abuse. Learn about the many programs in your community that encourage seniors to socialize, including senior center programs. Contact your local Area Agency of Aging (AAA) for more information (see listing in Appendix A).

Choose an Agent Carefully

Choose an agent (someone you choose who has the authority to act on your behalf) for a Financial Power of Attorney (a power of attorney that gives an agent authority to make financial decisions for you) that you trust, who is reliable, and who has your best interest in mind. You should hire an attorney to draft a financial power of attorney (see chapter 9).

Limit the Power Given to Your Agent

To avoid a potentially abusive situation, be very careful not to grant broad authority to your agent. Clearly state what rights you are granting and limit your agent's authority to what is needed. For example, if you only want someone to pay your bills from your checking account, only give your agent the right to access that account.

Abuse

Appoint a Monitor

Occasionally, agents misuse a Financial Power of Attorney by transferring property without paying a fair amount for the property or by trying to pressure or mislead you into a financial decision that is not in your best interest. Appoint a monitor to oversee your agent to ensure the agent is properly using his or her authority.

Be Careful of Joint Accounts and Other Accounts

Although joint bank accounts (a bank account that has two or more people who have the same rights to the account) are convenient, they are also risky. Both people have access to the money in the account. For example, if you have a joint account with your nephew and he fails to pay back a loan, the creditor can take the money from the joint account to satisfy your nephew's debt. There are better ways to allow people to manage your money. Talk to an attorney about an appropriate option for you. In addition, you should never let someone borrow your ATM card, credit card, or give them blank checks. Frequently monitor all your account statements and check your credit report annually. According to a recent study, Utah seniors lose around $52 million dollars a year due to exploitation.

Be Extremely Cautious in Deeding Real Property

Although there may be legitimate legal reasons for deeding your house to your children, it is not wise to do this while living and without legal consult. Once you have deeded your home, you no longer have the rights to live in it or sell it. While you may think that your children would never kick you out of your home, it does happen.

REPORTING ABUSE

How do I report abuse?

It can be difficult to report abuse, especially since abusers are often family members. However, no one should have to tolerate abuse, and you may have to report it to make it stop. If you are being abused, the most important thing you can do is tell someone you trust — a friend, a religious leader, a doctor, a family member, or Adult Protective Services (APS).

If you believe that another senior is the subject of abuse, neglect, or financial exploitation, Utah law requires you to report the abuse to APS or the nearest law enforcement office. If you fail to report abuse you could be charged with a misdemeanor (a lesser crime than a felony). Even if you are uncertain about the situation, it is best to err on the side of reporting the suspected abuse to APS.

APS is a government organization that assists vulnerable and elder adults in need of protection to prevent or discontinue abuse. All calls and reports are confidential.

MORE INFORMATION

ABUSE

Report any suspected abuse of a senior

Utah Adult Protective Services
800-371-7897
www.hsdaas.utah.gov

Information on abuse

National Committee for the Prevention of Elder Abuse
www.preventelderabuse.org

Chapter
4

CARING FOR GRANDCHILDREN

In This Chapter, Learn:

- How to form a Legal Relationship with Your Grandchild
- How to Enroll a Grandchild in School
- How to Get Visitation Rights
- How to Establish Kinship
- About Guardianship
- The Basics of Adoption
- About Much More

Grandchildren

39

CARING FOR GRANDCHILDREN

What should I know if I am caring for a grandchild?

It is common for parents to ask grandparents to care for their children while they are ill, on vacation, in jail, or simply not available. This could mean taking care of grandchildren for a few days or a few years. If this is the case, consider establishing a legal relationship so you have the authority to make medical, educational, and other decisions for your grandchild. Five types of legal relationships with your grandchild are discussed below — a delegation of parental powers, visitation, kinship, guardianship, and adoption. Each relationship establishes different authority and requires different responsibilities.

DELEGATION OF PARENTAL POWERS

Can I make decisions for my grandchildren if their parents are away?

Yes, if the parents give you the authority to do so through a "delegation of parental powers" document. This type of legal relationship is fitting

40

for those caring for their grandchildren for a few days or more.

What is a delegation of parental powers?

A delegation of parental powers is a legal document that a parent (or guardian of a minor child or incapacitated person) creates to give another person authority to make decisions. The parent still maintains all rights and responsibilities, but a delegation of powers gives another person the right to also make decisions regarding the child or ward.

Parents can give almost any power they want, such as the power to enroll a child in school or make a medical decision. However, there are some powers they cannot give, such as the power to adopt or consent to marry. Most often, parents create such a delegation so that if an emergency happens while they are gone, the grandparent has authority to make medical decisions for the grandchild.

This document is usually created when parents leave their children in the care of family members or friends for longer than a few days. A delegation of powers can last for any time period up to six months.

Do I need an attorney for a delegation of powers?

No, you can use a form that is available online at the Utah State Courts' Self-Help Resource Center (see the "More Information" section on page 48).

School Enrollment

How do I enroll my grandchild in school?

You can enroll a child in school with a delegation of parental powers document, guardianship, or custody agreement. In some cases, you may enroll your grandchild in school under the McKinney-Vento Act. This law states that a homeless child who is living with a relative on a temporary or emergency basis can be enrolled in school by that relative. The relative does not have to provide the necessary documents required for enrollment such as medical records, previous school records, birth certificate, and proof of residency. If you are using this law to enroll a child, ask to speak to the school's liaison for homeless children.

Visitation Rights

What are grandparent visitation rights?

Visitation rights are court-ordered rights given to grandparents to visit and spend time with their grandchildren. It is a legal remedy available under state law to grandparents who are being prevented from seeing their grandchildren.

How do I get visitation rights?

First, try to work out a solution with the parents without going to court. If that does not work, consider working with a mediator as soon as possible. Mediation is a great way to resolve family issues, especially at the beginning of a dispute. In mediation, both sides sit down with a mediator to voice concerns, listen, and come up with a resolution that is in the best interest of the parties. It often saves time and money, and it can do a lot to preserve family unity.

If mediation does not resolve the issue, you have the right to file a petition (written request) to the court asking for grandparent visitation rights. A grandparent may also file a petition in a pending (a case that has not been decided) divorce, custody, or visitation proceeding, asking for visitation rights.

Is it difficult to get visitation rights?

Yes, the court presumes that the parents' decision about visitation is always in the best interest of the grandchild until proven otherwise. Thus, grandparents will have to prove in court that visitation is in the best interest of the child. This is another reason why mediation is a preferred option.

The court will consider various factors in determining whether visitation is in the best interest of the child, such as whether:

- The grandparent is a "fit and proper person" to have visitation,

Grandchildren

43

- Visitation with the grandchild has been denied or unreasonably limited,
- The parent is unfit or incompetent,
- The grandparent has had a substantial relationship with the grandchild and the loss will harm the grandchild, and
- The parent of the grandchild has been missing from the child's life for an extended period of time because of death, divorce, or loss of custody.

KINSHIP CARE

My grandchild has been removed from the family home. Can he or she live with me?

Maybe. Kinship care is similar to temporary foster care. When children are removed from the parents' custody, a relative can care for the children on an emergency basis and possibly long-term. The purpose of kinship care is to reduce the trauma for the child by placing him or her with persons who are known and trusted.

For a child, to be considered for kinship placement, the relative must agree to a number of requirements, such as not allowing unauthorized contact with the parents or guardians, not discussing the events that led to removal, and providing information regarding the home environment of the placement. As always, the child's best interest is the most important factor.

Those who have kinship care can apply for financial and medical assistance for their grandchild (called a "specified relative grant") from the Utah Division of Workforce Services. This aid is not based on the grandparent's need, but on the child's assets (things that the child owns that have value) and income.

GUARDIANSHIP

How do I care for my grandchild for an extended period of time?

A legal guardianship is fitting if you are planning to care for a grandchild for an extended period of time. It is also a more fixed relationship as the parent cannot remove the child from the home without first going to court to terminate the guardianship.

A guardian is someone who is legally responsible for the care of another person. A guardianship gives those rights and responsibilities to a court-appointed guardian that are like those of a parent who has legal custody of a minor child. The parents retain their right and responsibility to support their child, the right to consent to adoption, the right to determine the child's religious affiliation, and the right to reasonable parent time — unless the court forbids it.

Grandchildren

How do I obtain a guardianship?

You file a petition with the court. The court will always consider the best interest of the child. The court may also consider whether the parents are alive, whether there was a nomination of a guardian in the parents' wills, whether the child was abandoned, or whether the parents consented to the guardianship. Gaining the parents' consent makes the process easier. If the parents have died or cannot be found, you must demonstrate this to the court. Parents have the right to contest the guardianship, which, makes the process more difficult.

Do I need an attorney to get a guardianship?

You don't need an attorney to petition the court for a guardianship; rather, you can do it on your own using the "Online Court Assistance Program" (OCAP; see the "More Information" section on page 48). If the guardianship is contested you are encouraged to hire an attorney.

What are my responsibilities as a guardian?

If you are appointed as guardian, you must provide the child with basic shelter, food, education, and clothing. You are not required to pay for the child's expenses out of your own funds. A legal guardian can also apply for public assistance to care for the child. Once you become a guardian, you must file an annual report with the court as long as the child is a minor (unless the guardianship was established only to enroll the child in school). For annual reporting forms go to the Utah State Courts' Self

Help Resource Center (see the "More Information" section on page 48).

ADOPTION

What is adoption?

When parents become unable to care for a child, grandparents will often want to adopt their grandchild. Adoption terminates the rights of the natural parents and gives full parental rights to another person.

Is it difficult to adopt a grandchild?

To adopt your grandchild, the natural parents' parental rights must be terminated. If the natural parents agree to the adoption, the process is much easier. However, if either parent contests the adoption, it is much more difficult because courts favor the parents' rights. Terminating parental rights to adopt in a contested matter requires a three-step process: (1) proving to the court that the natural parents are unfit; (2) demonstrating that it is in the best interest of the child to terminate the natural parent's rights; (3) and qualifying for adoption. In Utah, a hearing (a preliminary legal proceeding in court where you present your side of the case) is required to terminate parental rights.

47

MORE INFORMATION

GRANDPARENT

Seminars and support groups on grandparenting issues
Children's Service Society of Utah Grandfamilies Program
800-839-7444
801-355-7444
www.cssutah.org

Resources for grandparents caring for their grandchildren
AARP

www.aarp.org

Information on kinship care
Utah Division of Child and Family Services
801-538-4100
www.dcfs.utah.gov

Kinship financial assistance
Utah Department of Workforce Services
801-526-9675
www.jobs.utah.gov

MEDIATION AND VISITATION

Legal mediation for those with low and moderate income
Utah Dispute Resolution
877-697-7175
801-532-4841 (SLC)
801-689-1720 (Ogden)
www.utahdisputeresolution.org

GUARDIANSHIP

Information on guardianship of a minor
Utah State Courts' Online
Court Assistance Program
www.utcourts.gov

Utah State Courts' Self-Help Resource Center
www.utcourts.gov

Chapter
5

LEARNING ABOUT BENEFITS

In This Chapter, Learn:

- About Social Security Benefits
- How to Apply for Social Security
- How to Appeal Social Security Decisions
- About Veteran Benefits
- About Pensions
- What to Do if Your Pension is Denied
- About Much More

Benefits

Social Security

What is Social Security?

Social Security provides monetary benefits to workers who have retired, workers who have become disabled, and families of workers.

Am I eligible for Social Security retirement benefits?

 To be eligible for retirement benefits, there are two qualifications. First, you must be "insured" under Social Security. As you work and pay taxes, you earn Social Security "credits" for quarters of work. Most people need 40 calendar quarters, or 10 years of work to be fully insured for benefits. If you stop working, the quarters you worked will be on record and you may continue to accumulate credits if you work again.

Second, you must be at least age 62 and a U.S. citizen residing in the U.S. or a permanent noncitizen resident lawfully present in the U.S.

SOCIAL SECURITY RETIREMENT

How much will I get in Social Security retirement benefits?

The benefits you receive from Social Security depend on the amount you earn over your lifetime, your age at retirement, and other factors. The higher your income, the higher your benefits will be. To estimate your retirement benefits, ask the Social Security Administration (SSA) for a Social Security benefits statement or use the calculator on the SSA's website (see the "More Information" section on page 64).

At what age can I start receiving Social Security retirement benefits?

You may start receiving full benefits at age 65 or above (see chart below). If you need benefits earlier, you can receive them as early as age 62. However, if you retire early, your benefits will be reduced for as long as you receive them. For example, if you retire at age 62, your benefits could be reduced up to 30%.

At what age will I receive full Social Security retirement benefits?

The date for "full retirement" depends on your birth date. If you were born before 1938, you may take full retirement benefits at age 65. If you were born in or after 1938, the full retirement age is raised gradually until it reaches 67. For example, if you were born in 1939 you can retire with full benefits at age 65 years and 4 months (see chart).

Eligibility Year For Full Social Security	
Year Born	Full Retirement Age
1937 or earlier	65 years old
1938	65 and 2 months
1939	65 and 4 months
1940	65 and 6 months
1941	65 and 8 months
1942	65 and 10 months
1943-54	66
1955	66 and 2 months
1956	66 and 4 months
1957	66 and 6 months
1958	66 and 8 months
1959	66 and 10 months
1960 and later	67

Can I delay receiving Social Security retirement benefits?

Yes. If you choose to wait to receive benefits and continue to work beyond full retirement age, you will earn delayed retirement credits for the months you work. When you decide to receive your retirement benefits, your monthly benefit will be higher.

Can I receive Social Security retirement benefits and continue to work?

If you continue to work after reaching full retirement age, you will receive full Social Security benefits. If you choose to retire before reaching full retirement age, and you continue to work part-time, Social Security will reduce your benefits.

Social Security Family Benefits

What are Social Security family benefits, and am I eligible?

Family members may receive benefits based on the worker's eligibility for retirement or disability benefits. Family members eligible for these benefits include spouses, divorced spouses, and children. The discussion in this section presumes that the worker is living.

To be eligible, the worker must be entitled to receive benefits, and:

- A spouse must have been married to the worker for at least one year or be the natural parent of the worker's child, and be at least age 62 or caring for a child eligible for benefits based on the worker's account (minor under 16 or disabled).

Benefits

- A divorced spouse must not be eligible for equal or higher benefits under his or her own or another's Social Security record, must be at least age 62, must have been married to the worker for at least 10 years, and must be unmarried.

- Dependent children must be unmarried and under the age of 18 (or under age 19 if attending elementary or secondary school full-time). After age 18, a dependent child may receive benefits if he or she is disabled and the disability began before age 22.

SOCIAL SECURITY DISABILITY

What are Social Security disability benefits?

The SSA provides disability benefits under two major programs: the Social Security Disability Insurance (SSDI) program and the Supplemental Security Income (SSI) program. The following discussion will provide general information on both of these benefits. For specific information on your situation, you should contact your local SSA office.

Am I eligible for Social Security Disability Insurance (SSDI) benefits?

To be eligible to collect Social Security Disability Insurance benefits, you must be "insured" under Social Security. You must also be able to prove the severity of your disability, by showing that all of the following apply:

- You have a medically certified physical or mental disability.
- That disability prevents you from engaging in substantial gainful activity.
- The disability has lasted or is expected to last for at least 12 months or result in death.

SUPPLEMENTAL SECURITY INCOME

What is Supplemental Security Income (SSI)?

The Supplemental Security Income (SSI) program is based solely on need. It provides income to people who are 65 years and older or are blind or disabled. To qualify, receipients must have very limited income and resources and meet the requirements for citizenship or residency. A work history of amounts previously paid into the system is not needed to qualify. You may receive both Social Security Retirement (or Disability) benefits and SSI.

Am I eligible for SSI?

To be eligible for a SSI cash benefit, there are three qualifications:

1. You must be age 65 or older, blind, or disabled.

Benefits

2. You must have a limited income and resources.

3. You must also be a U.S. citizen residing in the U.S. or an eligible permanent non-citizen resident lawfully present in the U.S.

The definition of resources is complicated. It includes certain types of assets and excludes others. For example, the value of your home and your car are not deemed resources in calculating SSI eligibility. For more information on which resources are included and to see whether you qualify for SSI, you should contact your local SSA office.

Applying For Social Security

How do I apply for Social Security benefits?

SSA allows you to apply for retirement benefits three months before you are eligible or before you want to begin receiving benefits. If you are applying for survivor or disability benefits, you should apply promptly.

You may call your local Social Security office or SSA at 800-772-1213 to schedule an appointment to apply for benefits. For some Social Security programs, you may be able to apply online. You can also locate your local Social Security office by checking the SSA's website at www.ssa.gov. When applying, you must have the following documents:

- Your Social Security card or a record of your Social Security number.
- Your birth certificate or proof of your date of birth.
- Marriage certificate for benefits going to a spouse or children.
- Divorce decree for benefits going to your former spouse.
- Dependent child's Social Security number and birth certificate for benefits going to that child.
- Your W-2 forms and income tax return for the last year.
- Proof of U.S. citizenship or lawful residence in the U.S.
- If applying for survivor benefits, proof of worker's death.
- Name of financial institution and account number where you want to have your benefits deposited directly into your account.
- Military discharge papers if you served in the military.

If I cannot manage my finances, what happens to my Social Security?

If you are unable to manage your financial affairs, the Social Security Administration (SSA) must be advised that you need help. If it is in your best interest, the SSA will appoint a relative or a friend of yours, or

Benefits

may choose an institution, such as a nursing home, as the representative payee. A representative payee is a person or organization authorized to receive Social Security checks for someone who is unable to manage their own financial affairs. The SSA will notify you in writing if they appoint a representative payee.

APPEALING SOCIAL SECURITY

If I disagree with a Social Security decision, what can I do?

When a decision is made regarding your Social Security benefits or eligibility, the SSA will send you a letter explaining its decision. If you don't agree with a Social Security decision regarding your benefits, you have the right to appeal (a request to challenge the decision). You have 60 days from the date you receive the SSA letter to file your request in writing. Generally, if you don't appeal, the decision becomes final and you cannot appeal later.

What are the steps to appealing a Social Security decision?

In general, there are four steps to the appeals process, and there is a decision at each step. If you disagree with the initial decision, you typically have the right to move to the next step within 60 days of receiving written notice.

Reconsideration

You must file a written request for reconsideration of your claim within 60 days after receiving the initial decision letter. Someone at the Social Security Administration (SSA) who did not participate in the first decision will review your claim. Written notice of the reconsideration decision should be sent within 30 days (or longer if it concerns a disability claim).

Hearing

If you don't agree with the reconsideration decision, you may, within 60 days after receiving the decision, request a hearing before an Administrative Law Judge. The hearing may include witnesses, and you may have a representative assist you.

Appeals Council and Federal Court

For the last two levels of appeal, it is strongly recommended that you hire an attorney as these are technical levels of appeals.

VETERAN BENEFITS

What are veteran benefits?

The federal government offers to veterans of the United States Armed Forces and their dependents a broad range of programs and services provided

Benefits

by the Department of Veterans Affairs (VA). These benefits include health care, disability benefits, education programs, home loans, life insurance, burial, and survivor benefits.

Am I eligible for veteran benefits?

General eligibility for veteran benefits is based on being discharged from active military service under conditions other than dishonorable. Certain veteran benefits depend on individual circumstances. To determine eligibility, contact your local VA office.

What are the health care benefits for veterans?

The VA health care system is available to eligible veterans and includes hospitals, community clinics, nursing homes, counseling centers, and various other health care facilities.

What are veteran disability benefits?

The VA offers monthly disability compensation to veterans with a service-connected disease, disability, or injury sustained or aggravated during active military service. The amount of VA disability compensation varies according to the degree of disability and the disabled veteran's number of dependents. Military retirement pay and other separation payments may also affect the amount.

What are VA pensions?

Veterans with low incomes who are permanently disabled and are 65 years of age or older may be entitled to a pension benefit if they have 90 days or more of active military service with at least one day of service during a period of war. The pension provides a monthly payment to bring the veteran's total income to a level established by law. It may be reduced by other sources of income such as retirement or Social Security. (You should report all VA income to the SSA to avoid overpayment.)

What are veteran benefits for dependents and survivors?

The VA provides pensions to surviving spouses and unmarried children of deceased veterans. To be eligible, a spouse must not be remarried and a child must be under the age of 18 or under 23 if attending a VA-approved school, or permanently incapable of self-support because of a disability that began before age 18. This pension provides a monthly payment to bring the survivor's total income to a level established by law. The payment may be reduced by income from other sources such as Social Security.

Other benefits may be available to eligible veterans or their surviving spouses and children, including educational benefits, home loans, bereavement counseling, life insurance, medical care, and burial benefits. The burial benefits may include a grave site in a national cemetery, a headstone, a U.S. flag, and military funeral honors.

How do I apply for veteran benefits?

To apply for disability compensation and pension benefits, survivor benefits, or other veteran benefits, contact your local VA office.

Benefits

Pensions

What are pensions?

Pensions are private employee benefit plans set up by a company or by an employee or union agreement. If you have worked for a company that offered a pension, you may be entitled to a pension upon retirement.

There are minimum standards or rules for private pension plans established by federal laws. The most important federal law, the Employee Retirement Income Security Act (ERISA), covers most pension plans sponsored by companies and unions. ERISA does not cover plans sponsored by federal, state, and local governments, or religious organizations, which have their own rules.

How do I locate my pension plan?

If you believe that you are entitled to pension benefits and you are unable to locate the plan, or if you think the plan has been terminated, contact the Pension Benefit Guaranty Corporation (PBGC), a federal agency that insures benefit amounts to a certain limit. PBGC has a pension search directory listing people who are entitled to pension benefits but have not received them due to the funding company's inability to locate the individual. You can determine whether your benefits are insured by the PBGC by checking the company's summary plan description. To search the pension search directory, contact the

PBGC (see the "More Information" section on page 64).

Does social security affect my pension?

Under some plans, your pension benefits are "integrated" with Social Security benefits, which means that your pension payment could be lowered if you also receive Social Security. Under Federal law, such plans must provide you with at least half of your pension. This law applies only to years worked after 1988. For earlier years, your plan rules could leave you with no benefit after considering your Social Security payments.

What should I do if my pension is denied?

If you have been denied pension benefits, the pension plan administrator must inform you in writing and provide specific reasons for the decision. If you disagree with that decision and think you have been wrongfully denied benefits, you have the right to an appeal by the trustees of the plan. If you disagree with the decision by the trustees, you have the right to file a lawsuit in federal district court. Retaining an attorney who specializes in this area of law is recommended.

Benefits

MORE INFORMATION

SOCIAL SECURITY

Administers Social Security benefits

Social Security Administration
800-772-1213
www.ssa.gov

VETERAN BENEFITS

Administers various benefits to veterans

U. S. Department of Veterans Affairs
800-827-1000
www.va.gov

Assists veterans with preparing and filing claims

Utah Department of Veterans Affairs
800-894-9497
www.veterans.utah.gov

Disabled American Veterans
877-I-AM-A-VET (877-426-2838)
801-326-2375
www.dav.org

National Veterans Legal Services Program
202-265-8305
www.nvlsp.org

PENSIONS

Information regarding pensions and pension rules

Pension Rights Center
www.pensionrights.org

Regulates pension plans

Pension Benefit Guaranty Corporation
800-400-7242
www.pbgc.gov

Chapter
6

OBTAINING MEDICAL INSURANCE

In This Chapter, Learn:

- What Medicare Covers
- What Medicare Does Not Cover
- How to Apply for Medicare
- How to Appeal Medicare Decisions
- About Additional Supplemental Insurance
- About Medicaid
- Whether You Should Buy Long Term Care Insurance
- Where to Go for Health Insurance Advice
- About Much More

Medical Insurance

MEDICARE

What Is Medicare?

Medicare is a health insurance program for those 65 years or older, and people with certain disabilities, Lou Gehrig's disease, or permanent kidney failure.

For the purposes of this book we will be discussing three major types of Medicare. Each type (Part A, Part B, and Part D) has different eligibility requirements and provides different services. (See charts below).

How can I receive Medicare?

Participants can choose to receive their benefits straight from Medicare, or they can choose a Medicare Advantage plan (otherwise known as Medicare Part C).

Under Medicare Advantage you can choose to receive Medicare benefits from a private health insurance company such as a Preferred Provider Organization (PPO), a Medicare Medical Savings Account (MSA), Medicare Managed Care (ie, HMO), Medicare Special Needs Plan, or a private fee-for-service plan (PFFS).

Each Medicare Advantage plan must offer you the minimum Medicare benefits. Medicare Advantage plans may also offer various additional benefits. If you choose Medicare Advantage, please research which provider and plan is best for you.

MEDICARE BENEFITS

What are the Medicare benefits?

The charts below summarize the minimum benefits of Medicare Parts A, B, and D — eligibility requirements, premiums, and services covered and not covered. To get the most current information, contact Medicare (see the "More Information" section on page 88).

Medical Insurance

MEDICARE PART A

WHAT IS MEDICARE PART A?

• Hospital insurance

WHO IS ELIGIBLE?

You are eligible if at least one of the following describes you:

• You are at least 65 years old and eligible for Social Security or Railroad Retirement benefits.

• You have a disability and have been on Social Security disability or Railroad Retirement disability for the last two years.

• You are on dialysis because you have permanent kidney disease.

• You have Lou Gehrig's disease.

WHAT IS THE PREMIUM?

• Nothing, if you meet the eligibility requirements stated above.

• Around $248-$450 if you don't meet the eligibility requirements above.

MEDICARE PART A
WHAT DOES IT COVER AND
WHAT ARE THE DEDUCTIBLES?

	Deductible	Co-Payment (what you pay)
Hospitalization (semi-private room and board, general nursing, and other hospital services and supplies)	$1,132 in 2011	Days 1-60: no co-payment, just pay the deductible. Days 61-90: your co-payment is $283 a day. Days 91-150: (60 reserve days only used once) you pay $566 a day. Days 151+: you pay all costs.
Skilled Nursing Facility (semi-private room and board, skilled nursing services, inpatient drugs, physical, speech and occupational therapy)	None, but you must meet Medicare eligibility requirements for skilled nursing and therapies.	Days 1-20: no co-payment. Days 21-100: you pay up to $141.50 a day. Days 100+: you pay all costs.
Home Health Care (skilled care, home health aides, speech and physical therapy, durable medical equipment)	None, but you must meet Medicare eligibility requirements for home health care.	For services: no co-payment. For durable medical equipment: you pay 20% of costs.
Hospice Care	None, as long as doctor certifies the need.	Small co-payment for outpatient drugs and inpatient respite care.

Medical Insurance

MEDICARE PART B
WHAT IS MEDICARE PART B?
• Medical insurance that covers medically necessary doctor services, outpatient care, medical services, and some preventive services.
WHO IS ELIGIBLE?
• Same as Part A eligibility, and you must be a U.S. citizen or must have been a legal resident for at least five years.
WHAT IS THE PREMIUM?
• Your monthly premium is around $100 a month. Premiums increase yearly.

MEDICARE PART B

WHAT DOES IT COVER AND WHAT ARE THE DEDUCTIBLES?

	Deductible	Co-Payment (what you pay)
	$162, general deductible before any Medicare Part B benefits begin	
Medical Expenses (doctor visits, medical services and supplies, physical therapy, diagnostic tests, durable medical equipment)	None, if medically necessary.	General medical expenses: you pay 20% of the approved amount and limited charges above the approved amount. Outpatient mental health services: you pay 50%. Therapies have $1,870 per year limit for each type (speech, physical, and occupational).
Laboratory Tests	None, if medically necessary.	No co-payment.
Home Health Care (skilled care, home health aides, durable medical equipment)	None, but you must meet Medicare eligibility requirements for home health care.	For services: no co-payment. For durable medical equipment: you pay 20% of costs.
Outpatient Hospital Treatment (diagnosis or treatment services)	None, if medically necessary.	Billed Amount: generally you pay 20% (after the deductible).

Medical Insurance

MEDICARE PART D
WHAT IS MEDICARE PART D?
• Insurance for outpatient prescription medication.
WHO IS ELIGIBLE?
• Anyone who is eligible for Medicare Part A or is enrolled for Medicare Part B. • You may also qualify for "extra help" (from Medicare to pay for medication) if your assets and resources are below a certain amount. Contact Medicare for more information.
WHAT IS THE PREMIUM?
• It depends on the plan you choose.

MEDICARE PART D		
WHAT DOES IT COVER AND WHAT ARE THE DEDUCTIBLES?		
***(Please note due to the Health Care Act being passed changes are being made to Medicare Part D benefits)		
	Deductible	**Co-Payment (what you pay)**
The Basic Prescription Drug Plan	up to $310	After paying your deductible, you pay 25% and Medicare pays for 75% of your prescription drugs. When your total drug costs (including your deductible and co-payments) reach $2,840 or more, you pay 100% of your prescription drugs until your coverage begins again or until your total drug costs reach $4,550. When your total drug costs (including your deductible and co-payments) reach $4,550, you pay only 5% of your drug costs or a small co-payment ($2.50 for generics and $6.30 for brand-name drugs).

Medical Insurance

MEDICARE DOES NOT COVER

Read over the list below for specifics on what Medicare does not cover.

MEDICARE PART A DOES NOT COVER

Medicare Part A does not cover:

- Most nursing home care.

- Full-time home health care.

- Long-term care, including assisted living care, adult day care, and nursing home care (this is different than skilled nursing care).

- Personal care such as help dressing, bathing, and eating.

- Cosmetic surgery.

- Anything that is not reasonably and medically necessary.

- Care while traveling abroad.

MEDICARE PART B DOES NOT COVER

Medicare Part B does not cover:

- Acupuncture and homeopathy.

- Dental care and services.

- Routine physical examinations, unless it is an initial wellness exam or if it is an exam as part of a diagnosis for a medical condition or complaint.

- Vaccinations and immunization, unless you have been exposed or are planning to travel abroad.

- Eye and hearing exams; eyeglasses, contacts, and hearing aids.

- Routine foot care.

- Experimental procedures.

- Anything that is not reasonably and medically necessary.

MEDICARE DOES NOT COVER
MEDICARE PART D DOES NOT COVER

Medicare Part D does not cover:

• Barbiturates (sedatives, drugs used to treat anxiety and certain seizures).

• Benzodiazepines (tranquilizers, drugs used to treat panic attacks or seizure disorders).

• Over-the-counter medications.

• Weight loss or gain medications.

• Drugs for erectile dysfunction.

• Prescription vitamins.

Medical Insurance

What are some of the major changes made to Medicare Part D from the Health Care Act?

- In 2011 you will get a 50% discount from brand name drugs when you are in the coverage gap.
- Additional drug discounts by 2020.
- Eventually the coverage gap will shrink so you will only pay for 25% of costs.

APPLYING FOR MEDICARE

Do I need to apply for Medicare Part A or am I automatically enrolled?

It depends. If you are currently receiving Social Security retirement, you will be automatically enrolled in Medicare Part A. However, you need to apply for Medicare if you are not receiving Social Security.

When can I apply for Medicare Part A?

If you are not taking Social Security (see above), the soonest you can apply is three months before your 65th birthday. However, there is a seven-month enrollment period during which you can apply. It consists of the three months before the month of your 65th birthday, the month of your birthday, and three months following your birthday month.

When should I apply for Medicare Part B?

For Medicare Part B, the initial enrollment period is the same as Medicare Part A (see above). If you miss this enrollment period, you can sign up for Part B during the general enrollment period, which is between January 1 and March 31 of each year, with your coverage starting July 1.

What if I don't sign up for Part B when I am 65?

A 10% penalty is added to your premium for each full 12-month period that you could have had Part B but did not sign up for it. There is an exception. No penalty will be added if you had comparable group medical insurance. You will have to sign up for Medicare Part B while you have the comparable insurance, during the eight-month period that begins the month employment ends, or the comparable insurance ends, whichever is first.

APPEALING MEDICARE

What can I do if Medicare denies coverage?

Medicare is a very complex program. You might be denied a benefit when it should have been granted.

There may be times when Medicare decides that your stay in the hospital should end or they won't pay the amount you believe they should. Oftentimes this is because of an error.

You have the right to appeal (a request to change) Medicare decisions. How you appeal depends on whether you are appealing a decision under Medicare Part A, Part B, Medicare Advantage (Part C), or Part D.

For the purposes of this section we will only discuss the initial levels of appeals. Contact an attorney for more information.

How do I appeal traditional Medicare (Part A or Part B)?

When Medicare denies coverage under Part A or B, you will first find out from the health care provider and from a Medicare Summary Notice (MSN). Mistakes are often made due to insufficient information or simple mistakes. The first thing you should do is call the Customer Services Information number on the MSN.

How do I appeal a Medicare Part A or Part B decision?

You have 60 days from the date of the MSN to request an appeal, called reconsideration. You must request this in writing. The form will be provided with your MSN or you can print the form from www.medicare.gov/basics/forms.

If you don't appeal within 60 days, the decision becomes final and you cannot appeal later.

With the form, attach a letter to explain the situation. Be brief, but include the following key points: (1) what you believe Medicare should cover, (2) why it is medically necessary, and (3) why Medicare's decision was incorrect.

It is extremely helpful to have your doctor's support throughout the Medicare appeals process. This might be as simple as providing a copy of your medical bill and a letter from your doctor. Include these relevant documents with your appeal form and letter.

 If you disagree with the reconsideration decision, you should seek the help of an attorney to discuss whether you should appeal further.

How do I appeal a Medicare Advantage (Part C) decision?

If you receive Medicare A or B from a private insurance company, there is a different appeals process. The provider is required to provide you with information regarding their appeals process. In addition, every Medicare Advantage plan has internal grievance procedures for resolving issues.

First, you should ask the provider for a determination decision, in which the provider will decide whether they should have granted the benefit under Medicare. The provider must provide that decision in writing. Again, your doctor's support is essential to your appeal.

 If you disagree with the decision, you should ask for a redetermination, then seek the help of an attorney to discuss whether you should appeal further.

Medical Insurance

What should I do if my drug is not covered at the pharmacy?

First, check to see if the drug is excluded from Medicare Part D's coverage. (See Part D chart above.)

Next, ask your doctor if another drug on the plan's list would suffice. Provide him or her with the plan's formulary (the list of drugs that the plan covers).

Talk to your doctor about appealing to the plan so it will cover the necessary drug.

Pharmacists can also provide valuable information to patients and providers about why a certain drug in a class is better than another.

If necessary, appeal the provider's decision. Your doctor's and pharmacist's support is critical when appealing Medicare Part D.

How do I appeal Medicare Part D?

If you are denied coverage under Part D, you can appeal. This is called a "determination" appeal. If you disagree with the outcome you can appeal again. This section discusses the first three levels of appeals.

Determination

You should ask for a written coverage determination from your Medicare Part D provider. As part of your request, you will need your doctor to submit a statement that (1) the drug you need is medically necessary and (2) the alternative drugs on the drugs formulary would either not help or would harm you.

Submit as much information as you can that point to this fact. You may also want to include a letter from your pharmacist that explains why the drug you want is better for your treatment than another drug on the formulary.

After you request the coverage determination, your provider must respond within 72 hours. Your doctor can ask for an expedited review if your health requires. If you are granted an expedited review, your provider must make a determination within 24 hours.

Redetermination

Your doctor and pharmacist should submit statements with as much evidence as possible that your drug is medically necessary and that no other drugs will help you or that they would be harmful to you. This evidence can include medical records showing the other drugs you took were ineffective or had side effects which were harmful, and medical journal articles stating that the drug you want is effective in treating your condition. The more evidence you have, the better. Contact your provider to ask where you should send the request. You must ask for a redetermination within 60 days of the determination. The provider must respond to the redetermination request within 7 days, or 72 hours on an expedited review.

Reconsideration

If your redetermination is denied, you will receive a reconsideration appeal form. You must appeal within 60 days of receiving the form. Your doctor will have another opportunity to add any other medical evidence to support your case. Your reconsideration is looked at by a qualified independent contractor, who will consult doctors to help them make a decision. You should consider getting an attorney to help you at this stage of appeal. You will receive an answer within 7 days, or 72 hours on an expedited review.

 If you disagree with the decision you should seek the help of an attorney to discuss whether you should appeal further.

OTHER MEDICAL INSURANCE

Will Medicare cover all my costs?

Medicare was never intended to cover all medical costs. As you can see from the charts above, there are deductibles, co-payments, and areas that Medicare does not cover. After assessing your current and future health needs, determine whether or not to get additional health insurance. Research your options — Medicaid, Medigap, and long-term care insurance.

MEDICAID

What is Medicaid?

Medicaid is a health insurance program for individuals and families of low income and assets. Medicaid coverage is more extensive than Medicare. It includes hospital and medical services, prescription drugs, and long-term care such as nursing home stays.

To be eligible for Medicaid, you must fit one of the categories and your monthly income must be under 55% or 133% of the Federal Poverty Level, depending on the category.

Can I spend down so Medicaid will pay for my nursing home care?

Spending down is when you deplete your finances so that you become eligible for Medicaid. Spending down is confusing and a complex part of the law. The law on asset "transfers" and "gifts" has recently changed and is very technical. Making mistakes could prevent you from being eligible for Medicaid. If you are considering spending down, please talk to an attorney who specializes in Medicaid planning.

Medical Insurance

MEDIGAP

What is Medigap?

Medigap specifically helps pay for the expenses that Medicare doesn't, such as deductibles and coinsurance, and in some cases, may add additional benefits. (Medigap is good for people who have Original Medicare and not Medicare Advantage.)

There are a variety of Medigap plans. Some plans cover the gaps in Medicare for hospital insurance. Other plans may cover the gaps by providing coverage for skilled nursing care. The plan you choose depends on what coverage gap is most critical for you to have covered.

LONG-TERM CARE

Does Medicare pay for long-term care (LTC)?

 While Medicare pays for skilled nursing care, this coverage is very limited, and in general, Medicare does not pay for nursing home stays. Yet over 25 percent of those people who live to age 65 will eventually need some kind of long-term care.

Although your family might be able to provide part of the care for you, it is a huge financial strain. For example, the average care in a nursing home in Utah is $40,000 a year.

Should I buy long-term care (LTC) insurance?

The answers depends on your health and financial situation.

Generally, if you have more than $1.5 million dollars, you may be able to pay for LTC without a policy. If you have fewer assets, you may be able to spend down to qualify for LTC under Medicaid. Contact Senior Health Insurance Information Program (SHIP) counselors to help you determine whether you need LTC insurance (see the "More Information" section).

You should consider a LTC policy if you have no one in your family who could take care of your long-term care needs, you have a family history of disease that may require long-term care, and your assets are between $250,000 and $1.5 million.

What should I know about buying long-term care insurance?

Age

Unless you currently have a disability, the best time to get LTC insurance is between age 60 and 65. Policies get more expensive the older you get.

Premiums

Although premiums usually stay the same, companies can raise them under certain circumstances (e.g., inflation, losses, or changes in the law).

Medical Insurance

Care

When selecting a policy, buy one that covers in-home care (e.g., adult day care, home health care) as well as out-of-home care (e.g., assisted living, nursing home).

Benefits

Insist on a simple outline of the policy, which describes the benefits offered. Under law, this outline must be given to a person when you apply, pay for, or receive the policy.

Financial Strength

Before selecting a policy, find out the financial strength of the insurance company by going to www.standardandpoors.com.

Coverage

In Utah, the policy must cover custodial care (i.e., help with activities of daily living), Alzheimer's disease, and mental or nervous disorder of organic origin.

Benefit Period

Less than half of the people who are in a nursing home stay longer than 90 days, and if they do, almost all of them stay for less than 2.5 years. So think about averages like these when looking at the policy benefit period.

COUNSELING

Where can I get health insurance advice?

You can receive free Medicare counseling through your local Senior Health Insurance Information Program (SHIP). This program gives free local health insurance counseling to people who are eligible, or will soon be eligible for Medicare with their health insurance questions including the Medicare Prescription Drug Program. SHIPs are independent and not connected to any insurance company or health plan. SHIP volunteers work hard to help you with the following Medicare questions or concerns:

- Your Medicare rights
- Complaints about your medical care or treatment
- Billing problems
- Plan Choices

There is no charge for the service, and there is no product for sale. You can find a local SHIP counselor by calling 877-424-4640. If you're interested in becoming a volunteer SHIP volunteer, contact the SHIP in your state to learn more.

Medical Insurance

More Information

MEDICARE AND MEDIGAP

Free counseling on Medicare, Medigap, and long-term care insurance

Senior Health Insurance Information Program (SHIP)
877- 424 - 4640
www.daas.utah.gov

Utah Insurance Department, Health Insurance Division
801-538-3077
www.insurance.utah.gov

Information on Medicare

Medicare
800-MEDICARE (633-4227)
www.medicare.gov

MEDICAID PROGRAM

Information on Utah Medicaid

Utah Medicaid Program
800-662-9651
www.health.utah.gov/medicaid

LONG-TERM CARE INSURANCE

Information about long-term care

National Center for Assisted Living
800-628-8140
www.ncal.org

AARP
www.aarp.org

Chapter
7

FINDING HOUSING OPTIONS

In This Chapter, Learn:

- What Housing Is Available in Utah
- How to Choose the Right Housing
- How to Live Independently in Your Home
- About Home Health Care Agencies
- About Assisted Living and Continuing Care Retirement Communities
- How to Choose a Nursing Home
- About Your Nursing Home Rights
- About Much More

Options And Assessments

What housing options are available in Utah?

There are a variety of housing options available in Utah — from staying in your own home with assistance, to moving into housing designed for seniors, to moving into a nursing home with 24-hour care.

Which housing option should I choose?

People need housing options for many reasons. Sometimes they look for supportive housing assistance such as installing a handrail or hiring home care providers to assist with daily tasks like getting dressed. Other times people seek out housing for social interaction or skilled nursing services.

In determining the housing option that is right for you, assess your social needs, health needs, and financial situation. The chart below is a self-assessment tool to help you get started. You can also hire a professional to conduct an assessment.

HOUSING NEEDS ASSESSMENT	Y or N
SOCIAL NEEDS	
Do you want to live in your own home?	
Would you like to live near family and friends?	
Do you want to be more social or less social?	
Do you want to live in your community, near your church, doctor, beauty salon, bus stop, or grocery store?	
HEALTH NEEDS	
Can you clean your house and do your own yard work?	
Can you take care of your personal hygiene (comb your hair, brush your teeth, bathe, shave, and dress yourself)?	
Do you need help shopping?	
Can you prepare and eat your own meals?	
Can you drive?	
Do you need assistance taking your medications?	
Can you transfer from and to different places, such as from a bed to a chair?	
Do you need help either during the day or the night?	
Can you get around your house?	
Do you need assistance from a nurse or doctor?	
FINANCIAL SITUATION	
Can you balance your checkbook and pay your bills?	
How much can you afford to pay for housing and services that you need?	
If you don't have money available, are you willing to sell some of your assets to pay for care?	
Do you have long-term care insurance or health insurance that covers part or all of the costs of care?	
Do you have other resources available to help?	

Housing Options

What should I do after I assess my needs?

You should decide what type of housing suits your needs.

If you decide to stay in your own home, there are home modifications available, as well as supportive services and programs to make living in your own home safer and easier.

For some, staying in their current home is not possible. In that case, consider other settings like senior apartments, assisted living facilities, continuing care retirement communities, and nursing homes, which are described below.

LIVING IN YOUR HOME

Can I live independently in my home?

 As we age, most of us hope to continue to live independently. However, sometimes our home becomes unmanageable. We might not be able to walk up and down the stairs as we once did. We might need help with simple daily activities such as dressing, cooking, and bathing, or just want some social interaction. Or we might need skilled nursing care, but don't need a nursing home. If this is your case, there is good news. Years ago, people might have thought it was time for you to move to a nursing home, but not any more. Today, supportive services help seniors remain in their own homes. This can be as simple as help from family members to services provided by a local Area Agency on Aging (AAA), senior centers, nonprofit organizations, or for-profit businesses.

What services will help me live in my home?

Family and Friends

Ask your family and friends for help.

Area Agency on Aging (AAA) Programs

AAA programs are government supported services. For example, the Meals on Wheels program brings meals to those who are homebound. There are other programs that may make it safer and easier to continue to live in your home. Contact your local AAA for more information on availability and eligibility requirements. (See AAA listing in Appendix A.)

Senior Centers

Sometimes staying in your own home can make you feel lonely or isolated. Senior centers provide social and recreational activities, including a wide variety of free classes, programs, and meals.

Adult Day Care Centers

Seniors receive supervision during the day while receiving social, health, and recreational services they need at adult day care centers. In addition, these centers help seniors with their activities of daily living and provide meals and companionship.

Adult day care centers allow people to live at home with their families rather than at an assisted living

Housing Options

facility or a nursing home. Adult day care centers are a great option for caregivers who work during the day or need a break from caregiving.

Medicaid may pay for adult day care. Some long-term care insurance plans cover adult day care. Medicare will not pay for adult day care.

Homemaking Care

You can hire a homemaker who cooks, cleans, helps dress you, or provides transportation.

Home Modifications

Home modifications are another way of helping you stay in your own home. Some examples of modifications are grab bars in the shower, putting a bedroom on the main floor, a chairlift, a walk-in shower, or access ramps. Ask an occupational therapist or physical therapist from a home health agency to assist with recommendations for modifying your home to meet your needs.

Home Health Care

If you need help with personal or medical care, you can hire someone to provide those services in your home.

Home health care covers a variety of services including:

- Personal Care: Help with bathing, dressing, exercising, cooking, and hygiene.
- Health Care: Nursing, physical therapy, medical monitoring, rehabilitative therapy, and other medical assistance.

- Social Care: Transportation services and companions.
- Homemaking: Cleaning and shopping.
- Medical services: Skilled nursing care and rehabilitation therapies in your home.

How do I find a quality home health care agency?

When searching for a home health care agency, you might start by using the "Home Health Compare" search tool found online: www.medicare.gov. Next, ask your friends, relatives, and doctors for a referral. Once you have a recommendation, it is important that you ask the right questions before hiring the agency.

What questions should I ask a home health care agency?

- How long has the agency been in the business?
- Is it financially sound?
- What is the reputation of the agency in the community?
- What experience and certifications are employees required to have?
- Does the agency conduct criminal background checks and drug screening on its employees?
- Does the agency provide a home visit evaluation before providing services?
- Does the agency involve family members, doctors, and other specialists in the creation of a care plan?

Housing Options

- How often is the care plan reviewed?
- How does the agency ensure quality of care?
- Are there extra costs and fees, such as higher costs on weekends?
- Does the agency provide the services you need?
- Is there a doctor on staff?
- What is the response time of the agency for admissions and after-hour calls, and are they available for visits 24 hours a day?
- Is the agency and its staff Medicare certified?
- Does the agency have professional liability insurance?

How can I pay for home health care?

 Generally, Medicare only pays for short-term home health care if a doctor states that it is medically necessary, you are homebound or unable to live in your home without assistance, and you need one or more of the following services: intermittent skilled nursing care, physical therapy, speech therapy, or occupational therapy.

Some long-term care insurance plans may cover home health care. Medicaid may pay for home health care if you meet certain eligibility requirements. Some veterans may qualify for home health care under veteran benefit programs.

INDEPENDENT LIVING

What is independent living?

In the spectrum of senior housing options available, independent living is in the middle. It is for those who cannot or don't want to live at home, but who don't need a nursing home. You still have some of the freedom and comfort of home, but you also have some of the personal care and medical services of a nursing home. Even better, with independent living, you don't have the high costs of a nursing home.

There are two major types of independent living communities — senior residences and assisted living facilities.

What is a Senior Residence?

Seniors typically have their own apartment. Seniors pay for their own rent and may purchase additional services offered if needed. It is a great place for seniors who want to socialize and still have amenities close by. This type of housing is specifically designed for seniors. They have handrails, elevators, ramps, and other senior-friendly modifications. The residence provides some meals and social and recreational activities. Sometimes they have a bank, hair salon, bookstore, and other shops in or near the facility. They even have laundry, homemaking, and housekeeping services available for an additional fee. If you need help with activities of daily living such as bathing, dressing, cooking, and eating, you may be able to

Housing Options

97

live in a senior residence and hire a home health agency to provide personal care services.

If you have a low or moderate income, you may qualify for government-subsidized senior housing. Most subsidized senior housing communities offer meals and activities during the day. Contact your local AAA for more information (see listing in Appendix A).

What is an assisted living facility?

Assisted living facilities are for those who cannot live by themselves but who don't need nursing home care. They provide the comforts of home with as much independence as possible, while providing extensive supportive services.

Residents of assisted living facilities live in their own apartment and may or may not have a roommate. Meals are provided in a common dining room. Residents may need very little assistance or may need help with administration of medications, bathing, dressing, transferring out of bed, laundry, and housekeeping.

Assisted living facilities also track a resident's health and medical condition and can help with monitoring the resident during the day and night, and administering medication and medical aids such as oxygen. The facility provides activities and may have housekeeping services available at an additional cost.

At these facilities, you pay rent and additional fees for services you need.

HIGHER LEVELS OF CARE

What is a continuing care retirement community (CCRC)?

These are retirement communities that offer all levels of care from independent living to assisted living to nursing home care. Residents can move from a lower level of care to a higher level of care as needed or receive services in their own home. This allows seniors to age in place. That is, they never have to move out of the facility because they need a different type of care. This is an expensive type of long-term care as residents may have to pay an entrance or buy-in fee in addition to the monthly fees. This entrance fee can range from $38,000 to $400,000. Before moving into a CCRC, be sure to have an attorney look at the contract the facility will ask you to sign.

What is a nursing home?

A nursing home is the highest level of care other than acute care in a hospital. Sometimes people are there for a short time while they recover from an illness or injury. At other times people are in a nursing home for a long period due to a serious illness. The staff provides 24-hour nursing care for those who can no longer care for themselves but don't need hospitalization. A doctor supervises the care of the patient. The nursing home hires a number of skilled professionals such as nurses, physical therapists, speech therapists, and occupational therapists to provide care.

They also provide meals, activities, and personal care. Medicare will cover the initial costs of skilled nursing and rehabilitative care, but will not cover long-term care needs or custodial care (see chapter 6).

How do I choose a nursing home?

 Find out what nursing homes are in your area and whether they provide quality care. There are several places you can go to determine this: Medicare's website, Health Insight, state inspection reports, your local Ombudsman, and your own research and evaluation.

Medicare's Website

The government has an online website called "Nursing Home Compare" which is found at www. medicare.gov. It provides statistics that might alert you to nursing homes that have serious quality-of-care issues. It also provides information on the number and type of health deficiencies, fire safety deficiencies, and nursing home staff-to-resident ratios.

Health Insight

Health Insight is a nonprofit organization dedicated to improving Medicare quality of care. They use the state inspection reports to rank the best and worst nursing homes. They also give annual awards to nursing homes that exhibit high quality of care.

State Inspection Reports

The Utah Department of Health inspects each nursing home yearly and writes a state inspection report summarizing violations and residents' complaints. Each nursing home is required to make its state inspection report available to the public. Usually nursing homes have the form posted in their lobby or in a folder marked "state survey." If it is not available, ask management for their state inspection report. When reviewing these reports, look for serious violations.

Ombudsman

The Long-Term Care Ombudsman program helps protect the rights of residents of long-term care facilities, including nursing homes and assisted living facilities. The Ombudsman investigates and mediates complaints made by those 60 and older who live in a facility. They can also help you access and interpret state inspection reports, and they provide you limited advice on evaluating nursing homes.

Your Own Research and Evaluation

To determine the facility's quality of care, you will have to conduct your own research. Just like when you buy a car, you should not rely solely on information from the salesman. Research and talk to residents, aging professionals, the Ombudsman, and others before you select a nursing home.

Look for a facility that promotes independence and a home-like atmosphere, allows the resident or their family to be involved in decision-making, and

Housing Options

encourages outside visits. Research indicates that facilities that have a higher daily average of care from nurses have a higher quality of care than other facilities.

The following list may be useful to determine a quality nursing home:

VISITING A FACILITY	Y/N or ✓
LOCATION	
Is the facility near your family so they can visit often?	
REFERENCES	
Ask family, friends, the Ombudsman, and aging professionals about their experiences with the facility.	
COSTS	
Ask about costs, accepted insurance, and penalty costs.	
What services cost extra?	
QUALITY OF CARE	
What are the staff- and nurse-to-patient ratios?	
What services are offered?	
Can the resident use his or her own doctor?	
What are the rooms like?	
Can family and friends visit anytime?	
Is there a nice private place to visit with residents?	
Is there a bed hold fee?	
Is there a nurse, doctor, and social worker at the home at all times?	
Do they require criminal background checks on employees?	
What types of complaints have they received from residents?	
Do they offer the services you need?	
OBSERVATIONS	
Visit the facility more than once. Try to visit during late morning or midday when residents and the staff are interacting.	
How does the facility seem when you walk in? Does it feel more like a hospital or a home?	
Is the facility clean? Are there odors?	
Is the facility crowded?	

Housing Options

VISITING A FACILITY	Y/N or ✔
OBSERVATIONS (continued)	
Ask to see inspection reports for the last couple of years.	
Is the staff friendly and patient?	
How much privacy will the resident have?	
Are residents clean and properly groomed?	
Does the staff know their residents' names?	
Talk to residents and their families. Are they pleased with the nursing home?	
Do they have a variety of meal choices?	
Are there security issues?	

What are my nursing home rights?

 As a resident of a nursing home, you have certain rights under the Federal Nursing Home Reform Act. A nursing home is required by law to provide you with written information regarding your rights. Generally, residents have the following rights:

The Right to Information

- Medical records.
- Resident status and medical condition.
- Costs of all services.
- Facility reports and correction plans conducted by the government.

The Right to Self-Determination

- Choose one's own doctor.
- Be free from physical and mental abuse.
- Be involved in one's treatment plan.
- Right to make an advance health care directive.

The Right to Be Visited

- By family and friends.
- By a physician of one's choosing.
- By the State Ombudsman and other government representatives.

The Right to Privacy

- Send and receive mail.
- Have access to a telephone.
- Have private visits with family, friends, the State Ombudsman, and other government representatives.
- Have medical records kept confidential.

Every Resident Has the Right to Make Complaints

- Without fear of reprisal.
- To the Ombudsman about the nursing home or to report abuse.
- To file a lawsuit.

MORE INFORMATION

HOUSING OPTIONS

Information about housing options

Senior Housing Net
www.seniorhousing.net

Eldercare Locator
www.eldercare.gov

Products that help people live independently

Life Solutions Plus
www.lifesolutionsplus.com

SENIOR CENTERS

List of Utah seniors centers

Utah Division of Aging and Adult Services
www.hsdaas.utah.gov

NURSING HOMES

Information on specific nursing homes

Medicare
800-MEDICARE (633-4227)
www.medicare.gov

Health Insight
www.healthinsight.org

Inspects nursing homes

Utah Department of Health
www.health.utah.gov

Investigates complaints at nursing homes

Ombudsman Program
Contact local Area Agency on Aging
    (see listing in Appendix A).

Chapter
8

ORGANIZING YOUR ASSETS: ESTATE PLANNING

In This Chapter, Learn:

- Whether You Should Have a Will or Trust
- What Happens if You Don't Have a Will
- Whether You Need an Attorney to Create a Will
- About Probate
- What are the Benefits of a Trust
- About the Dangers of Joint Accounts
- About Much More

WILLS

What is a will and what does it do?

A will is a document that states how you would like your property distributed after your death.

In a will, you typically:

- Appoint a person, called a personal representative, who carries out the instructions in your will.
- Identify the people or charities that are to inherit your assets.
- Make special provisions, such as naming a person you would like to act as guardian for your minor children or adult children with a disability.

Do I need a will or a trust?

It depends. Your estate plan should be customized to fit your needs and objectives. A will, a trust, or both can be designed for many purposes, such as property management, assistance in the event of incapacity (lack of mental or physical capacity), and disposition of property after death. Discuss your needs and objectives with an attorney.

What if I don't have a will when I die?

This is called dying "intestate." If this happens, your assets will go to your heirs according to state law. Generally under Utah law, if your spouse survives you, he or she will inherit everything. However, if you have children who aren't your surviving spouse's

Estate Planning

children, then your surviving spouse receives $75,000 plus half of the remainder of your estate. The rest of your estate is divided equally among all your children. If you have no surviving spouse, your assets are divided among your heirs (i.e., children); if you have no children, the assets go to the surviving parents. If you have no surviving parents, your property goes to your siblings or their children.

Do I need an attorney to create a will?

You are strongly encouraged to hire an attorney to create a will. A skilled attorney will ensure that your will clearly states your desires in a way that complies with the law. That said, you can handwrite your will, as discussed below.

I recently moved to Utah. Do I need a new will?

No. It is wise, however, to have an attorney in Utah review your will. They can look to see whether Utah laws will affect your will and suggest changes, if necessary.

Should I write my own will?

Some people use computer software, a pre-printed form, or handwrite their own will. However, this is risky. These methods often produce a will that is unclear or does not comply with Utah law and that can result in a fight between your heirs over who gets what. This type of litigation is often very expensive and time consuming and can permanently tear families apart. We do not recommend that you write your own will. Start the right way and hire an attorney to draft your will.

What if I still want to draft my own will without an attorney?

Despite knowing the risks, some people still want to draft their will without an attorney. While not advisable, Utah law does recognize a holographic (handwritten) will.

For a holographic will to be valid in Utah, (1) the entire will must be in your handwriting (not typed on a computer), and (2) you must sign and date the will.

If you are determined to draft a holographic will, here are some suggestions of what to include. These suggestions might not fit your particular circumstances, but they will give you a starting point for creating a holographic will.

- State that you intend this to be your will and you are revoking all prior wills.
- State your name and address.
- Name a personal representative.
- Identify your spouse and all your children.
- Describe all your property and assets.
- Clearly state which person gets what assets.
- Number the pages of the will.
- State that you are waiving the requirements of a bond for the personal representative.
- Sign and date the will.

Who should I choose as a personal representative?

 Your personal representative is responsible for gathering, managing, and distributing your assets under your will. Choose someone you trust to follow your wishes and who is willing to act as your representative. Beneficiaries (those who receive or are to receive something of value) can become emotional regarding the property distribution, so it's important to choose a personal representative who will follow your instructions regardless of the pressure the beneficiaries try to put on them.

PROBATE

What is probate?

Probate is a process by which the court determines the validity of the will and officially empowers the personal representative to act. The personal representative:

- Gathers the assets of the decedent.
- Applies the assets to pay debts, taxes, and expenses of administration.
- Transfers the remaining assets to the beneficiaries named in the will.

What assets don't go through probate?

The following is a partial list of property that may pass outside your probate estate unless you make the estate the beneficiary:

- Retirement accounts such as IRAs and 401Ks, life insurance proceeds, and employee death benefits go to the beneficiaries you have designated in those accounts or policies.
- Assets held in "joint tenancy."
- Assets held in a trust.
- Accounts that are "payable on death" go to the designated person.
- Certain small estates (see below).

Should I try to avoid probate?

Probate is not as cumbersome and costly as it once was. The average time it takes to probate a will is between four months and one year, depending on the size of the estate, the complexity of transferring the assets, and whether the will is contested. The average cost of probating a simple, uncontested estate when an attorney is involved is between $1,500 to $2,500. Be careful of those over-exaggerating the costs of probate.

What if I don't have a lot of assets, do I have to go through probate?

A small estate affidavit may be an option. In Utah, if an estate is worth $100,000 or less and does not include real estate, probate may not be necessary. In this case, the successor of the estate can use an affidavit (a written statement made under oath) to collect the deceased person's property. The affidavit must state that (1) the value of the estate subject to probate does not exceed $100,000; (2) thirty days have elapsed since the deceased's passing; (3) no application of a personal representative is pending or has been granted in any jurisdiction; and (4) the claiming successor is entitled to payment or delivery of the property.

TRUST

What is a trust?

A trust is a document in which you appoint someone to manage assets for you and any designated beneficiaries.

In a trust you appoint a trustee to manage the assets. You can appoint yourself or another person. If you name yourself, you should also name a successor trustee to take over upon your death or if you don't have mental capacity.

What are the benefits of having a trust?

There are benefits to creating a trust (so long as all your assets are in the trust).

Assets held in a trust:

• Don't go through probate.

- Avoid the need to appoint a conservator.
- Allow you to state the circumstances under which your beneficiaries will receive the trust assets.

Shouldn't everyone have a trust?

 While trusts are a valuable estate planning tool, they are not for everyone. For instance, it is not always a good option for those with a small estate. Despite this, there are salespeople who use scare tactics to get seniors to create trusts. They may state that a trust will save you thousands of dollars, guarantee that the government won't take your property, ensure that your heirs receive your estate, and avoid costly probate. These statements are not true for everyone. Some salespeople are not qualified to create a trust but may draft your trust anyway, or they may neglect to transfer your property into the trust.

 Even if your estate is modest, there are many estate planning options that will ensure that your assets are distributed as you wish. Before determining which estate plan is best for you, examine all estate planning options with an experienced estate planning attorney.

UPDATING ESTATE PLANNING

When should I update my estate planning?

 You should update your estate planning when you experience a life change. This could include a new marriage, birth, adoption, or divorce. To help you think about the potential impact on your finances and the changes you need to make, answer the following questions:

- Do you want to change the beneficiaries to your will or trust, such as including a new spouse or child?

- Do you want to revise the assets and properties that you are leaving to your beneficiaries?

- If you are getting married, do you want to protect your assets for your children's inheritance and at the same time provide for your new spouse after your death?

- Do you want to change the name of your executor, agent, or personal representative?

- If your assets have increased or decreased since the last review, do you want to change how those assets are distributed?

TAXES

Should I worry about estate taxes?

If your estate will be worth $1 million dollars or more when you die, you should talk to an estate planning or tax attorney about your estate tax liability (debt or legal responsibility). Tax planning is very complicated, and tax laws change frequently.

When do I have to pay a gift tax?

Generally, any time you make gifts worth more than $12,000 to one person (other than your spouse) in any given year, you must file a gift tax return. You can give as many gifts as you would like as long as the total amount of the gifts don't exceed $12,000 per person per year. There are a few other exemptions, such as payments for medical care or education. If you plan to make gifts of more than $12,000 to any one person in a year, talk to an estate planning or tax attorney first.

PROPERTY

Should I deed my house to my kids now to avoid probate costs later?

 We strongly advise against deeding your house for several reasons. You will no longer own it, your heirs may have to pay more in taxes if you deed it over, and it may make you ineligible later for Medicaid.

If you transfer your house to your children, they will own the house. This transfer can have unforeseen consequences. For example, if your child defaults on a loan, the creditor could force the sale of the home since your child holds the deed to the house. Also, your child, as owner of the house, could decide to evict you. Second, there may be gift tax issues. If you deed the house over to your children, they will have to pay capital gains on the home's original value. So if you bought your home for $100,000 and it is now worth $300,000, and you deed it to your children, they would have to pay capital gains taxes on $200,000 (the difference between the original value and the current value). However, if you gave them the house through your will and they then sold it for its current value of $300,000, they would not have to pay capital gains tax. Third, transferring your house for less than its value may make you ineligibile for Medicaid. There are better ways to transfer your house to your child. Talk to an attorney for more details.

What is a life estate?

A life estate is ownership of property that terminates on your death. Here is an example of how a life estate works. Paul owns a cabin in the Uinta mountains. He marries Jenessa. Later, he dies. In his will he gives Jenessa a life estate to the cabin and the future interest of the cabin to their children, Hugo and Nola. This means that Jenessa can live in the cabin until she dies. Upon Jenessa's death, Hugo and Nola inherit the cabin.

If Jenessa decides that she wants to sell the cabin, she cannot sell the property completely because she only owns the cabin until she dies. After that, Hugo and Nola own it. If Jenessa sells her life estate to Lyman, Lyman can use the cabin while Jenessa is living. Once Jenessa dies, the property goes to Hugo and Nola.

If you hold a life estate, you cannot damage or devalue the property. However, you can make improvements as long it does not devalue the property.

What about owning property together?

When buying property with another person, be sure to identify whether you are holding the property as joint tenants or as tenants in common.

In joint tenancy, when one joint tenant dies, the property passes to the surviving joint tenant automatically. For example, if Paul and Jenessa own a house in joint tenancy, and Paul dies, Jenessa now owns the entire house. Married couples typically choose to own property in joint tenancy because it is easier to pass property to the surviving spouse.

In tenancy in common, each owner has a share of the property that he or she may sell without the other's consent. The share of each tenant in common passes as provided in a will and is subject to probate.

My son is helping me pay my bills. Should I put his name on my checking account?

Probably not. When you add someone to your checking account, you are creating a joint account. There are some advantages to setting up a joint account, as it permits a second person to help out with paying bills and managing your money. However, as a result, two people can withdraw money even if only one of them is depositing money into the account. This may lead to unexpected and unwanted results. For instance, let's say that you have a joint account with your son. If your son defaults on his car loan, the creditor can seize the money in the joint account. While you can sue your son for the money taken from the joint account, this situation can be difficult to resolve.

What is the best way to leave my bank account to someone upon my death?

The best way to leave your checking account to someone after your death is by creating a "payable upon death" account. This form, available from your bank, allows you to name a person who is to inherit the money upon your death.

MORE INFORMATION

ESTATE PLANNING

Information on estate planning

Utah State Bar
www.utahbar.org

American Bar Association
www.abanet.org

Chapter
9

KEEPING THE POWER:
END-OF-LIFE PLANNING

In This Chapter, Learn:

- About Advance Health Care Directives
- About a Health Care Power of Attorney
- About a Living Will
- About the Importance of Choosing the Right Agent
- How to Create a Health Care Power of Attorney
- How to Create a Living Will
- About Guardianships
- About Conservatorships
- About Much More

ADVANCE HEALTH CARE DIRECTIVES

What is an Advance Health Care Directive?

An Advance Health Care Directive, also called an "Advance Directive," is a legal document that describes your end-of-life health care wishes. In Utah, the Advance Directive is a form with four parts:

Part I. Health Care Power of Attorney

This part allows you to appoint another person called a health care agent to make health care decisions if you are unable to make decisions or speak for yourself.

Part II. Living Will

This part allows you to express directly to health care providers your preferences regarding life-prolonging medical procedures.

Part III. Revocation

This part allows you to revoke or change an Advance Directive.

Part IV. Execution

This part makes the document legal. This part requires your signature and that of a witness.

You don't have to complete all parts of an Advance Directive. For example, you can fill out Part I but not Part II of the form.

Do I need an Advance Directive?

 You can benefit from having an Advance Directive at any age. You could have an accident or get sick. In the future you could have a mental or physical illness that leaves you without the ability to make decisions.

Making an Advance Directive allows you to direct how decisions should be made if you can no longer communicate your wishes. This keeps the focus of decision-making on you and your wishes.

What is a health care agent?

A health care agent is a person you appoint to make medical decisions for you in the event you are unable to make them for yourself.

How should I choose an agent?

 Choosing your agent is one of the most important things you do when creating a Health Care Power of Attorney. It is important to choose an agent whom you trust because your agent will carry out your wishes when you are unable to make or communicate decisions. You should also choose an alternate agent in case your agent is unable or unwilling to serve.

What should I tell my agent?

You should have a discussion with your agent about any current, serious medical conditions, specific health care preferences, and general thoughts you have about end-of-life care. To help you get started with this discussion, download a copy of Utah's

End-of-Life Planning

Toolkit for Advance Health Care Planning (see the "More Information" section on page 134). If you fill out a Toolkit or worksheets, you should give your agent a copy, along with your Advance Directive.

What powers can I give my agent?

Your agent has broad powers to make medical decisions for you, including:

- Consenting to, refusing, or withdrawing any health care treatment.
- Hiring and firing health care providers.
- Asking questions and getting answers from health care providers.
- Consenting to admission or transfer to a medical provider or facility.
- Getting copies of medical records.
- Asking for consultations or second opinions.

You can give your agent additional powers, if you choose, including:

- Getting copies of your medical records even if you can communicate your health care decisions.
- Authorizing organ donation.
- Admitting you into a facility such as a nursing home.
- Other powers not contained in Utah's form on the blank lines provided in Parts I and II.

When do an agent's powers begin?

Your agent's powers begin when you cannot make or communicate health care decisions for yourself.

The law requires a finding by a physician or in some cases a physician assistant or a nurse practitioner that you lack capacity to make a health care decision.

How do I express end-of-life care wishes?

Part II of Utah's Advance Directive lets you document your end-of-life care preferences. You can choose whether you want medical procedures that prolong life or not. If you don't want to prolong life, you can choose at what point you want to withdraw life-sustaining treatment.

Do I need an attorney to create an Advance Directive?

No, you don't need to hire an attorney to create an Advance Directive. The form discussed in this section was designed for use by the public.

You can download the Advance Directive Form from Utah's Division of Aging and Adult Services (see the "More Information" section, page 134).

Should I complete a new Advance Directive if I already have one?

If you created an Advance Directive before 2008 that was legally valid, it is legally valid today. However, a new law was passed in 2008 that covers more circumstances than the older form. Everyone who can should complete the new form.

What should I do after I sign my Advance Directive?

Keep the original Advance Directive and worksheets or other notes where your agent can get the original document, if needed.

Give your agent a copy of the Advance Directive plus any worksheets or notes. Make sure your agent knows where to find the original. Also, give copies to other family members or friends who may have to make a medical decision for you if your agent is not available.

Give your doctor a copy of your Advance Directive. Ask for it to be included in your medical record. Make sure your doctor will support your wishes.

When should I update my Advance Directive?

Review your Advance Directive once a year or when an event changes your life. Think about the '5 Ds' to decide when you should change or update your Advance Directive. The 5 Ds are: decade birthday (40th, 50th, etc.), diagnosis of a new illness or condition, deterioration of health, divorce, and death of somebody close to you.

What if the doctor won't follow the Advance Directive?

While you can sue in court to enforce the directive, the easiest way to resolve the situation is to work with the hospital (customer service or risk management) or to get a different doctor.

Do EMTs have to follow my Advance Directive?

No. EMTs are not trained to follow Advance Directives. If EMTs are called, their primary task is to keep you alive until you get to the hospital. If you don't want emergency providers to perform CPR, you must work with your health care provider to complete an order on a form approved by the Utah Department of Health.

GUARDIANSHIP

What is a guardianship?

A guardianship is a court-ordered arrangement through which one or more persons, called guardians, are legally authorized to make decisions for another person, called a ward.

When is a guardianship necessary?

Sometimes people become incapable of making minimally adequate decisions about medical treatment, everyday life, or other important matters and there are no voluntary arrangements through which the person can be assisted in making adequate decisions. As a result, their health and safety are in jeopardy. Under Utah law, when this happens, a court may appoint a guardian to make decisions for that person.

What are the responsibilities of a guardian?

Under a limited guardianship, a guardian may only make those decisions that the court has authorized the guardian to make.

Under a full guardianship, the guardian is generally responsible for:

- Determining where the ward lives.
- Making sure that the ward's basic needs are met.
- Protecting and advocating for the ward's rights.
- Making decisions about the ward's health care and treatment.
- Keeping track and taking care of the ward's property and possessions.
- Making some financial decisions for the ward, if the ward does not have a conservator.
- Reporting to the court annually about their guardianship activities, the condition of the ward, and the status and condition of the ward's estate.

Who can become a guardian?

Any competent adult and some agencies can be appointed as a guardian. The law gives preference, however, to appointment of the following persons in the following order:

- Persons suggested by a ward, in the event the ward is capable of expressing a preference.
- Close family members of the ward.

How is a guardianship established?

 Any person who believes that another person needs a guardian may file a petition for appointment of a guardian in state court. Usually an attorney represents the person filing the petition and another attorney represents the proposed ward. A doctor or psychologist may examine the proposed ward to determine if the person has capacity to make decisions and care for themselves.

After receiving a petition, the court schedules a hearing. Various interested parties, including the proposed ward, must be notified of the hearing. If the proposed ward does not have an attorney or cannot afford one, the court will appoint one to represent the proposed ward. At the initial hearing the judge may schedule a trial, or if the judge finds no opposition to the petition, the judge may grant the petition. At the conclusion of the hearing or trial, the judge or jury decides whether or not to grant the petition.

What is a conservatorship?

A conservatorship is like a guardianship, but only for finances. The conservator has authority to make financial decisions on your behalf.

Under a full conservatorship, the conservator is generally responsible for:

- Using the protected person's income and financial resources to provide for the person's care, support, and comfort and to pay the person's bills and debts.

- Keeping track and taking care of the protected person's property and personal possessions.
- Investing or selling the protected person's assets and property, if needed.

What are some of the alternatives to guardianship and conservatorship?

 Because guardianship limits a person's ability to make decisions for himself or herself, it should always be used as a last resort. Some decision-making tools and voluntary arrangements that may be used as alternatives to guardianship include:

Money Management Services

Banking services, such as direct deposit and direct payment, may help you if you are having difficulties keeping track of your money and paying your bills.

Representative Payee

If you are unable to manage your financial affairs, the Social Security Administration (SSA) can appoint a relative, friend or institution as the representative payee.

Advance Health Care Directive

An Advance Directive is a legal document that you can create to inform others how you want to be cared for in the event you become incapable of making medical decisions.

Trusts

A trust is a legal arrangement in which a person or institution called a trustee holds title to property for your benefit or the benefit of another person. Trusts can be a very helpful option when planning for incapacity.

POWER OF ATTORNEY

What is a power of attorney?

A power of attorney is a legal document in which you give a person, called an agent, the authority to act on your behalf. For instance, you can give someone the authority to sell your home, pay your bills, or buy groceries for you. The person who grants the power is called a "principal" and the person who is given the authority is the "agent."

What authority does the agent have under a power of attorney?

You decide what authority to give your agent. You can give the agent limited authority to pay your bills, for example, or you can give general power to make any day-to-day decisions, as well as business and legal decisions. You should give your agent only the authority you want them to have.

When can my agent act?

This depends on the type of power of attorney you set up. There is a springing power, nondurable power, and durable power of attorney.

Springing Power of Attorney

The agent receives authority at a specific time or when a specific event occurs (such as when the principal becomes incapacitated or lacks mental capacity).

Nondurable Power of Attorney

The agent receives authority as soon as the principal creates the power of attorney, and it is revoked if the principal becomes incapacitated, dies, or revokes the power of attorney.

Durable Power of Attorney

The agent is authorized to act even after the principal becomes incapacitated.

What is the most important thing to know about a power of attorney?

You should select your agent with care. Your agent should be someone you completely trust. Talk to any prospective agent before you appoint them to make sure he or she is willing to be your agent. It is wise, especially with a Financial Power of Attorney, to appoint a monitor that watches over the agent. The monitor ensures the agent is acting in your best interest.

How do I create a power of attorney?

Creating a power of attorney is not a "one size fits all" situation. You should hire an attorney to create a power of attorney that fits your specific needs. However, you don't need to hire an attorney to create a Health Care Power of Attorney.

What is a Financial Power of Attorney?

A Financial Power of Attorney gives your agent specific authority to make finance-related decisions.

What is the most important thing to know about a financial power of attorney?

You should select your agent with care. Power of attorneys can be misused as they have little built in safeguards to protect you. So it is critical not only to pick an agent that you completely trust but also to appoint a monitor that watches over your agent and your accounts. The monitor should have no power to move assets or make decisions. The monitor's job is only to watch over your account to ensure your agent is acting in your best interest and is not misusing or stealing from your account. Your agent and monitor should be people that you completely trust. Talk to any prospective agent before you appoint them to make sure he or she is willing to be your agent.

What if I don't have a durable financial power of attorney?

There may come a time in life where you are unable to handle your finances. This could be due to incapacity of some sort (e.g. dementia). If you don't have a durable financial power of attorney, your relatives or loved ones will have to go to court to appoint a conservator or guardian to manage your finances. This type of proceeding can be costly as it requires that both parties have an attorney. Sometimes the court hearing is contested and causes family strife. This doesn't mean that you should run out and get a durable financial power of attorney. Since an agent under a financial power of attorney has the potential to exploit, you first want to make sure you can appoint an agent you trust as well as a monitor to audit the agent (see chapter 3).

MORE INFORMATION

ADVANCE HEALTH CARE DIRECTIVES

Advance Health Care Directive form, toolkit, and instructions

Utah Division of Aging and Adult Services
877-424-4640
801-538-3910
www.hsdaas.utah.gov

GUARDIANSHIP AND POWER OF ATTORNEY

Information online regarding guardianship, conservatorship, advance directives, and power of attorney

Utah State Courts' Self-Help Resource Center
www.utcourts.gov/howto

Information about guardianships

Office of Public Guardian
www.opg.utah.gov

Chapter 10

MAKING ARRANGEMENTS: DEATH OF A LOVED ONE

In This Chapter, Learn:

- What to Do Immediately After Someone Dies
- What Tasks Can Wait
- What Documents to Gather
- How to Obtain a Death Certificate
- About Much More

Priority of Tasks

What tasks need to be handled?

Some of these tasks require more immediate attention than others.

This might be overwhelming. You don't need to do everything yourself. Look for a friend, close family member, or the personal representative who is named in the decedent's will to assist you with some of these tasks. It may be best to postpone any decisions that can wait until you are feeling better emotionally.

For example, the decision to sell the home should be made carefully only when you are emotionally ready.

First Day

What should I do first?

The decisions made during the first week are typically decisions made by the close family members.

Please read the will as it may or may not assign specific people to be involved in these tasks.

Immediately Notify the Appropriate Person about the Death

If your loved one dies at home and the death was expected, then simply notify the physician and the chosen funeral home. If the death was unexpected — for example, a death by violence, suicide, drug overdose, poisoning, or suspicious accident — then you are required by law to call the police. If your loved one dies in a hospital or nursing home, notify a nurse or other staff member.

Make a Decision Regarding the Decedent's Organs

Check to see whether the person wished to donate their organs. There are three ways in which people can state they are organ donors:

- They can register on the organ donation list (one can register when applying for a Utah driver's license or ID card).
- They can state it in their will.
- If they have a terminal illness or injury, they can tell two people they want to donate their organs (one person has to be a disinterested party).

If the decedent (a person who has died) did not express specific wishes regarding organ donation, certain family members may need to make this decision. In Utah, there is a priority list of people who can give consent: the agent of the donor who could have made the decision before the decedent's death, the surviving spouse, adult children, parents, adult siblings, adult grandchildren, grandparents, and guardians, in that respective order.

Contact Family Members and Close Friends

• Start informing family members, friends, and other relevant persons regarding the passing.

Make Arrangements for Children and Pets

• Check the will to see whether there are any instructions regarding who should care for children and pets.

First Week

What should I do in the first week?

Plan the Funeral

You should contact the funeral home during the first 24 hours. The funeral home will be able to help you make arrangements for transporting the body to the funeral home. Ask the funeral home for a price list. According to the Federal Trade Commission, any time prices are discussed you must be presented with a complete price list of goods and services the funeral home offers.

Find out the decedent's burial and funeral wishes. Again, look to the will or other documents to determine these wishes. Also, consult family members regarding the wishes of the decedent. If the deceased was on public assistance, funds for an indigent (someone of lower income) burial or cremation may be available (varies depending on the county).

Use Veteran Benefits for Funerals

Generally, if the deceased was a veteran, the Department of Veteran Affairs will provide at no cost a U.S. flag, a grave site in a National Veterans' Cemetery, a headstone, and military funeral honors. In addition, some veterans may be eligible for burial allowance that gives partial reimbursement for burial and funeral costs. Contact the Department of Veteran Affairs for more information.

FIRST MONTH

What should I do within the first month?

During the first month, the personal representative can handle a lot of the following tasks. Family members may provide direction or handle these matters until a personal representative is designated or appointed by the court. Tasks include gathering important documents, obtaining death certificates, making a list of the decedent's assets, preserving property, and notifying others.

What documents should I gather?

Before dealing with benefit, legal, and financial issues, you will need to gather a variety of important documents:

- Wills
- Trust agreements

- Deeds
- Mortgages and title policies
- Stock and bond certificates
- Account statements
- Bank statements and checkbooks
- Certificates of deposit
- Insurance policies
- Divorce papers
- Motor vehicle titles and registrations
- Lease agreements
- Marriage, birth, and death certificates
- Annuities
- Social Security numbers
- Recent income tax returns and recent W-2 forms
- Military records
- Retirement and brokerage accounts (IRA, 401K, 403(b), pension)
- Partnership and corporate papers

How do I obtain a death certificate?

A certified copy of the death certificate will be needed each time you are asked to provide "proof of death." You may be asked for proof of death when transferring the title of property, filing insurance claims, accessing certain property, and applying for various types of benefits.

The quickest way to obtain a copy of the death certificate is from the funeral director. You should obtain at least 5 to 10 certified copies of the death certificate. The certificate can also be obtained directly from the Utah Department of Health's Office of Vital Records.

Who should make a list of the decedent's assets?

If you are the personal representative or acting until one is appointed, try to locate and prepare a list of what the deceased owned.

How should I preserve the property?

Make sure that the decedent's assets are safe and secure. For example, make sure the decedent's property taxes are paid and that the house is locked and properly insured. Unfortunately, some thieves target homes of people who have recently died, so make sure that the house is secure. If there is a vehicle, make sure it is in a safe place.

After contacting family who else should I notify?

The following is a list of individuals whom you should contact at an appropriate time.

Employer

Contact the deceased's employer to make arrangements for any last pay check. Survivors may be able to receive benefits from a pension plan, life insurance, and 401K.

Post Office

Mail for the deceased should be marked "deceased — return to sender" or forwarded to the person taking care of the deceased's mail.

Life Insurance Agent

To make a claim for death benefits, talk to the insurance agent where the deceased's policy was held.

Business and Financial Institutions

When your loved one dies, you should cancel services and subscriptions. You should also notify any financial institutions (e.g., banks, brokerage services, credit card companies) where the decedent conducted business. If the decedent had a joint account, have the decedent's name taken off the account.

Social Security Administration

If the decedent was receiving Social Security benefits, you must report the death to the Social Security Administration by calling 800-772-1213. You also must return any check or payment received for the month of death.

If the decedent was eligible for Social Security benefits, a family member may be eligible for death and survivor benefits (see chapter 5 for more information about Social Security).

Tax Advisor

You might have to prepare and file the decedent's tax return. Contact the deceased's accountant or your own tax advisor.

Attorney

If applicable, contact an attorney to help with the legal steps necessary to handle the estate.

Health Insurance Company

Notify the health insurance company of the death and provide them with a death certificate. Arrange to have the deceased persons name removed from the health insurance policy while keeping others covered on the policy.

Veteran Administration

If the deceased was a veteran notify the veterans agency so they can stop any payments that they may have been making. The Veterans Administration may also offer benefits for funeral or burial costs.

More Information

ORGAN DONATIONS

Registry for organ and tissue donation

Utah Donor Registry
866-937-8824
www.yesutah.org

DEATH CERTIFICATES

Order official Utah death certificates

Utah Department of Health, Office of Vital Records
801-538-6105
www.silver.health.utah.gov

FUNERAL TRADE RULES

Information on the funeral trade rules

Federal Trade Commission
877-FTC-HELP (382-4357)
www.ftc.gov/funerals

Chapter
11

GETTING LEGAL HELP:
WHERE TO GO FROM HERE

In This Chapter, Learn:

- Where to Go for More Legal Help
- About Solving the Issue Yourself
- How to Get Brief Legal Help
- How to Hire an Attorney
- About Much More

SOLVING THE PROBLEM YOURSELF

Where do I go for more information?

Now that you are armed with an improved knowledge of the law, you are better able to navigate the issues that face people 55 and over. Search out resources in the "More Information" sections of each chapter, go to the library and bookstores, go to a recommended website, or take a class.

How do I resolve a dispute?

If your issue involves a dispute with another person or organization, try to resolve the dispute. If you are unable to resolve the issue, see whether the organization or person is willing to go to mediation. Mediation is a great way to resolve disputes without having to go to court. Some mediation services are affiliated with the courts, while there are also private and nonprofit mediation services. A mediator acts as a neutral person who listens to both parties and tries to move them to an acceptable resolution. You can find a list of mediators, and more information about mediation services, at the Utah State Courts' Self-Help Resource Center website (see the "More Information" section, page 151).

Can I sue in small claims court?

You can file a consumer claim (such as a breach of a contract, property damage, consumer complaint, or payment owed) against a person or a business if your claim is not above $10,000. The rules in small claims court are simple, and you can file and present your case without an attorney. For a guide on filing a small claims case, go to the Utah State Courts' Self-Help Resources website.

Can I represent myself?

There may be a time when you are unable to hire an attorney and will need to represent yourself, or maybe you just need more information about how the court works. The Utah State Courts have an excellent Self Help Resource Center online. It has pro se (representing yourself) packets, how-to guides, and legal forms. It also provides a wealth of information on different areas of law (see the "More Information" section, page 151).

Legal Help

GETTING BRIEF LEGAL HELP

Where can I get a legal question answered?

Salt Lake and Washington County have free legal clinics staffed by volunteer attorneys for seniors of all income levels. These clinics specifically address elder law issues. Each appointment lasts about 20 minutes. You tell the attorney your problem, and he gives you his legal assessment. Your conversation with the attorney is confidential, but the attorney is not representing you. In addition, there are free legal clinics all over the state where people of low income can go for brief legal advice. For a list of clinics, go to the Utah State Courts' Self-Help Resources website (see page 151).

What are government legal services?

In Utah, the government funds limited legal assistance to those 60 years and older. Those who are in the greatest social and economic need are given priority in receiving services. Typically cases involve guardianship, Advance Health Care Directives, consumer fraud, housing issues, and long-term care rights, among others.

These legal services also include community legal education and legal advice. In some very rare cases, representation might be available. For more information on this resource, call your local Area Agency on Aging (AAA) (see listing in Appendix A, page 157). The AAA is the government organization that provides aging services in your local community. They can direct you to the legal service provider they contract with in your area. Most often they will refer you to the Senior Legal Helpline at Utah Legal Services.

HIRING AN ATTORNEY

How do I hire an attorney?

Although hiring an attorney may be costly, sometimes it is necessary. If cost is an issue, try to find an attorney who offers unbundled legal services. This allows you to hire an attorney for limited representation. You choose exactly what legal tasks you want the attorney to perform. For example, you could hire an attorney to just draft a document, review a document, or represent you through a legal issue.

 One way to find an attorney is by asking friends, family, and professionals in the field for a recommendation. It is very important to hire an attorney who specializes in the area of law surrounding your legal question. For example, you should hire an attorney in estate planning or elder law if you have a question about a trust. Conversely, you should not hire a tax attorney for a family law issue.

Before hiring an attorney, make sure you ask the following questions:

- How long have you been practicing law?
- What is your area of expertise?
- How much do you charge?
- Is there a charge for the initial consultation?

- Have you ever had a bar complaint? (You can confirm this with the Utah State Bar.)
- How long does it take you to return a client's phone call?
- How long will my case take?
- What outcome can I expect?

MORE INFORMATION

MEDIATION

Provides mediation in small claims courts and for those with low and moderate income

Utah Dispute Resolution
877-697-7175
801-532-4841 (SLC)
801-689-1720 (Ogden)
www.utahdisputeresolution.org

SMALL CLAIMS AND PRO SE

Information on filing a small claims suit

Utah State Courts' Self-Help Resource Center
www.utcourts.gov

Online assistance for filing pro se documents

Utah State Courts' Online Court Assistance Program
www.utcourts.gov

CLINICS

Free legal clinics on elder law

St. George Legal Clinic
St. George Senior Center
245 North 200 West
435-634-5716 (by appt. only)

Salt Lake Senior Legal Clinics
Held at Various Senior Centers
Utah State Bar (call for specific locations and times)
801-297-7049

Provides a list of free legal clinics throughout Utah

Utah State Courts' Self-Help Resource Center
www.utcourts.gov

GOVERNMENT LEGAL SERVICES

Provides free brief legal advice to vulnerable seniors

Senior Legal Helpline (funded through 2012)
9 am – 2 pm
800-662-1772

Provides legal advice, information and representation to low income Utahns

Utah Legal Services
801-328-8891
800-662-4245
www.andjusticeforall.org/uls

HIRING AN ATTORNEY

Provides a lawyer referral service

LegalMatch
www.utahbar.legalmatch.com

To check for complaints against an attorney

Utah State Bar
801-531-9077
www.utahstatebar.org

GLOSSARY

Adult Protective Services: Utah government organization that assists vulnerable and elder adults in need of protection to prevent or discontinue abuse, neglect, or exploitation until that condition no longer requires intervention.

Advance Directive: a form that allows you to (1) choose an agent to make health care decisions for you when you cannot make decisions for yourself, and (2) allows you to state your end-of-life health care wishes.

Affidavit: a written statement made under oath.

Agent: someone you choose who has the authority to act on your behalf.

Appeal: taking the case to a higher court or level to request a change in the decision.

Assets: things that one owns that have value.

Beneficiary: one who receives or is to receive something of value.

Conservator: someone the court appoints who has the authority to act on your behalf to make financial decisions for you.

Contract: a legal agreement between two or more parties.

Decedent: a person who has died.

Deed: a legal document that gives someone title to real property.

Default: a legal failure to do something.

Estate: property that a person owns or possesses.

Exempt: released from a liability.

Felony: a serious crime.

Financial exploitation: using a person's assets, money, or property to deprive that person of using, benefiting, or possessing that property.

Financial power of attorney: a power of attorney that gives an agent authority to make financial decisions for another.

Guardian: one who has legal custody to make decisions for another person.

Hearing: a preliminary legal proceeding where you present your side of the case.

Holographic will: a handwritten will.

Incapacitated: lack of mental or physical capacity.

Indigent: someone who is poor or of lower income.

Joint bank account: a bank account that has two or more people who have the same rights to the account.

Joint tenancy: when two or more people own property together. If one dies, the other automatically inherits the property.

Liability: a debt, legal responsibility, duty, or obligation.

Mediation: resolving a conflict between two or more parties by meeting with an impartial person called a mediator.

Misdemeanor: a lesser crime.

Pending: awaiting a decision.

Pension: a retirement benefit plan set up by a company or employer.

Personal representative: the person who carries out the instructions in your will.

Petition: a written request to the court.

Physical abuse: harm to a person that causes injury or will likely cause injury.

Power of attorney: a legal document where you give a person called an "agent" the authority to act on your behalf.

Probate: the process the court goes through to validate a person's will, appoint a personal representative, gather a person's assets, pay any debts and taxes, and oversee the transfer of assets to the beneficiaries.

Representative payee: a person or organization authorized to receive Social Security checks for someone who is unable to manage his or her own financial affairs.

Trust: an entity that owns, holds, and manages assets for the benefit of another.

Trustee: the person or organization that manages the assets and property in a trust.

Will: a legal document that states how you would like your property distributed after you die.

APPENDIX A
GOVERNMENT AGENCIES

UTAH DIVISION OF AGING AND ADULT SERVICES

The Division administers a wide variety of home and community-based services for Utah residents who are 60 years of age and older. Programs and services are primarily delivered by a network of 12 Area Agencies on Aging, which reach all geographic areas of the state. Their goal is to provide services that allow seniors and vulnerable adults to remain independent.
877-424-4640
www.hsdaas.utah.gov

UTAH ASSOCIATION OF AREA AGENCIES ON AGING

An Area Agency on Aging (AAA) is a local government agency that provides services, advocacy, assistance, and answers to the elderly and their caregivers. These agencies serve as a focal point for linking people with information, nutrition, supportive services, and concerns regarding the elderly. Links to various Utah county agencies on elder care are provided. For information contact the AAA in your county.

Counties: Box Elder, Cache, Rich
Bear River Area Agency on Aging
435-752-7242 or
877-772-7242
www.brag.utah.gov

County: Davis
Davis County Bureau of Health Promotions and Senior
Services
801-451-3377
www.co.davis.ut.us

Counties: Beaver, Garfield, Iron, Kane, Washington
Five County Area Agency on Aging
435-673-3548
www.fcaog.state.ut.us

Counties: Summit, Utah, Wasatch
Mountainland Dept. of Aging and Family Services
801-229-3800
www.mountainland.org

County: Salt Lake
Salt Lake County Aging Services
801-468-2454
www.slcoagingservices.org

County: San Juan
San Juan County Area Agency on Aging
435-587-3225
www.sanjuancounty.org

Counties: Juab, Millard, Piute, Sanpete, Sevier, Wayne
Six County Area Agency on Aging
435-893-0700
www.sixcounty.com

Counties: Carbon, Emery, Grand, San Juan
Southeastern Utah Area Agency on Aging
435-637-4268 or 5444

County: Tooele
Tooele County Div. of Aging and Adult Services
435-882-2870
www.co.tooele.ut.us

Counties: Daggett, Duchesne
Uintah Basin Area Agency on Aging
435-722-4518
www.ubaog.org

County: Uintah
Council on Aging/Golden Age Center
435-789-2169
www.co.uintah.ut.us

Counties: Morgan, Weber
Weber Area Agency on Aging
801-625-3770
www.weberhs.org

Appendix B
Nonprofit Agencies

AARP Utah Office
866-448-3616
www.aarp.org
Provides information on various aging topics.

ALZHEIMER'S ASSOCIATION Utah Chapter
800-272-3900
www.alzutah.org
Provides support groups, referrals, workshops, and seminars offered throughout Utah. Check their website for dates and times.

DISABILITY LAW CENTER
800-662-9080
800-550-4182 (TTY)
www.disabilitylawcenter.org
Provides advocacy and legal assistance free of charge to eligible clients. DLC handles cases concerning the abuse and neglect of people with disabilities, accessibility, housing discrimination, special education, and other issues relating to the rights of people with disabilities.

ELDERCARE LOCATOR
800-677-1116
www.eldercare.gov
Helps identify resources to enable seniors to live independently in their local area.

LEGAL AID SOCIETY OF SALT LAKE
801-328-8849
www.lasslc.org
Provides free legal assistance on family law and domestic violence issues for low-income people.

UTAH LEGAL SERVICES
801-328-8891
800-662-4245
www.andjusticeforall.org/uls
Provides free legal services to low-income families and individuals, as well as seniors.

UTAH STATE BAR
801-531-9077
www.utahbar.org
Organizes free legal clinics, including legal clinics for seniors.

Appendix C
Acknowledgments

This book was made possible by:

Utah Division of Aging and Adult Services

The Borchard Foundation Center on Law and Aging

Bank of American Fork

Ballard Spahr LLP

Special thanks to:

Sharon M. Bertelsen, Attorney, Ballard Spahr LLP

As with any book there are good days, and days of challenges and hurdles. While others shied away from difficulties, Sharon helped me face these challenges head on. Sharon's optimism and attitude of putting seniors first paved the way to success. Her exuberance, unstinting support, and belief in this publication were astounding; without her this project would not have been possible.

The following people were also instrumental in ensuring the success of this book:

Dan Hogan, Owner, Sheridan Publishing

Nels Holmgren, Director, Utah Division of Aging and Adult Services

Alan K. Ormsby, AARP Utah State Director

Professor Edward D. Spurgeon, Executive Director, The Borchard Foundation Center on Law and Aging

Thanks also to:

Maureen Henry, Director, Utah Commission on Aging; Donna Russell, Director, Utah Office of Public Guardian; Kevin Olsen, former Director, Utah Division of Consumer Protection; and Nels Holmgren, Director, Utah Division of Aging and Adult Services, who generously allowed us to reprint some of their materials as part of this book.

Focus groups throughout Utah.

Those who provided advice, writings, and edits who wished to remain nameless.

This book would not have been possible without the generous help of many attorneys, social workers, and professionals who volunteered their time and expertise in reviewing, providing technical advice, editing, and other help. On behalf of Utah's Department of Human Services, I thank them for their service and support. These individuals' encouragement and feedback were invaluable to this process.

- Kent B. Alderman, Elder Law Attorney, Parsons Behle & Latimer
- Fred W. Anderson, Attorney
- Kris Atkinson, R.N.
- Kathleen Bailey, former State Ombudsman, Utah Division of Aging and Adult Services
- Lois Chatfield, focus group participant
- Mary Jane Ciccarello, Attorney, Assistant Director, The Borchard Foundation Center on Law and Aging
- Jane Clayson, freelance editor
- Gina Coccimiglio, Owner, CareSource Home Health and Hospice

- Mario Colosimo, Integration Coordinator, RIESTER Advertising

- Margot Dana, Attorney; Rehabilitation Supervisor, Utah Division of Rehabilitation Services and Work Ability

- Rebecca Davis, Attorney, Pension Rights Center

- Larry Dawson, Veterans Outreach Representative, Utah Department of Veterans Affairs

- Barbara J. Dieker, Director, Office of Elder Rights, U.S. Administration on Aging

- Chuck Diviney, former Information Specialist, Utah Adult Protective Services

- Kathryn Draper, Executive Secretary, Utah Division of Aging and Adult Services

- Jane Driggs, President, Better Business Bureau of Utah

- Jeffrey Duncan, Bureau Director, Office of Vital Records and Statistics, Utah Department of Health

- Autumn Fitzgerald, Attorney, Fitzgerald & Fitzgerald Attorneys at Law, LLC

- Carolyn Geigle, Office Technician, Utah Division of Aging and Adult Services

- Robert Gordon, Office Technician, Utah Division of Aging and Adult Services

- Sarah Graham Halsell, Attorney, State Legal Services Developer, State of Florida

- Janelle Gunther, Ph.D., Consultant

- Elisabeth Guyon, Copy Editor

- Judy A. Hall, C.O.T.A./L, Kindred Healthcare, District Director for Sales Development

- AnnaLisa Hernandez, Children's Service Society of Utah, Grandfamilies Program

- Tressa Hiddenfriend, freelance professional proofreader

- Caroline Hobson, focus group participant
- Ann Hopkins, Director, CHRISTUS St. Joseph Villa
- Darren Hotton, Senior Health Information Insurance Program Manager, Utah Division of Aging and Adult Services
- Nobu Iizuka, Ombudsman, Weber Area Agency on Aging
- Keri Jones, Chief Program Officer, YWCA Salt Lake City
- Jansen Gunther, Law Clerk, University of Virginia
- Kris Knowlton, Assistant Attorney General, Utah Office of the Attorney General
- Joellen Leavelle, Communications and Outreach Coordinator, Pension Rights Center
- Christopher Liechty, Office of Christopher Liechty & Sons, Graphic Designers
- Margene Luke, VA Hospital
- Peggy Matlin, Program Manager, Utah Division of Aging and Adult Services
- Cory Maxwell, Director of Publishing, Deseret Book Company
- Scott McBeth, Director, Mountainland Department of Aging and Family Services
- Muffy Mead-Ferro, Cardon-Ferro Creative, LLC
- Edward R. Munson, Attorney, Jones Waldo Holbrook & McDonough, PC
- Daniel Musto, State Ombudsman, Utah Division of Aging and Adult Services
- Kevin V. Olsen, former Director, Utah Division of Consumer Protection
- Holly Robinson, former Associate Staff Director, American Bar Association Commission on Law and Aging

- Michael Rubin, Project Analyst and Coordinator, Center for Medicare Advocacy

- Will Shinen, former Law Clerk, Clinical Program, S.J. Quinney College of Law

- David Stevens, freelance book designer

- Diane Stewart, former Director, Utah Adult Protective Services

- University of Utah Osher Lifelong Learning Institute, Law and Aging classes

- Alisa Van Langeveld, Ph.D, Associate Instructor, University of Utah

- Richard S. Victor, Executive Director, Grandparents Rights Organization

- Olene S. Walker, former Governor of Utah

- Rick Warne, Assistant Professor, George Mason University

- Lee Ann Whitaker, Office Specialist, Utah Division of Aging and Adult Services

- Stephanie D. Whittier-Ellis, Program Specialist, Office of Elder Rights, U.S. Administration on Aging

- Tammy Wood, Health Program Manager, Utah Division of Aging and Adult Services

- Kari Stonely Uitto, PharmD, Clinical Pharmacist

- Sonnie Yudell, Caregiver Program Manager, Utah Division of Aging and Adult Services

Index

A

AARP 4, 18, 48, 88, 161
Abuse 31-38, 105
Abusers 31, 32
Adoption 39, 47, 115
Adult Protective Services 37, 38, 153
Advance Directive 122-127, 130, 134, 153
Affidavit 112-113, 153
Agent 35, 36, 115, 123-125, 131-133, 151
American Bankruptcy Institute 30
American Bar Association 120
Annual Credit Report Request Service 7, 16
Appeal 49, 58, 59, 63, 65, 77-82, 153
Area Agency on Aging 93, 106, 148, 157-159
Assets 107-120
Assisted Living 74, 88, 89, 97, 98
Attorney 4, 21, 23, 24, 28, 35, 36, 41, 46, 59, 63, 78, 79, 82, 83, 99, 108, 109, 110, 114, 116, 118, 125, 129, 132, 142, 147, 148, 149-150

B

Bankruptcy 19, 27-28
Better Business Bureau 12, 18, 20, 29

C

Certified Mail 11, 27
Children's Service Society of Utah 48
Collection 19, 26-27
Complaint 8, 10, 12, 17, 18, 19, 20-22, 105, 106, 152
Conservator 114, 121, 129, 130
Continuing Care Retirement Community 92, 99
Contract 11, 19, 23-24, 99, 151, 153
Contractor 1, 2, 12-13, 18
Creditor 8, 27, 28, 36, 117, 119
Credit Report 7, 8, 16, 36

D

Death 44, 55, 108, 112, 113, 115, 118, 119, 135, 137

Death Certificate 135, 144
Debt 15, 19, 26-27
Decedent 111, 136, 137, 138, 139, 141, 142, 153
Deductible 69, 71, 73, 84
Deed 34, 36, 37, 117-118, 140, 153
Delegation of Parental Powers 40-41
Demand letter 20-22
Determination 79-82
Direct Marketing Association 9, 17
Disabled American Veterans 64
Dispute 19, 20, 25, 27, 43, 48, 146, 151
Door-to-Door 11, 18, 21
Durable Power of Attorney 131, 132

E

Eldercare Locator 106, 161
Eligibility 50, 52, 53, 60, 61, 68, 70, 72-83, 139
End-of-Life 121-134
Equifax 16
Estate 107-120
Estate Planning 4, 107-120
Execution 122
Exempt 28, 116, 151
Experian 16

F

Federal Communications Commission 10, 17
Federal Trade Commission 5, 8, 10, 16, 17, 18, 29, 138, 144
Felony 37, 152, 154
Finances 13, 57, 83, 115, 129, 133
Financial Exploitation 31, 34-38, 154
Financial power of attorney 35, 36, 132-133, 154
Foreclosure 4-5
Funeral 61, 135-144

G

Grandchild 39-48
Guardian(ship) 4, 39, 40, 45-48, 108, 121, 127-130, 133, 134, 137, 148, 154

H

Health Care Directives 122-127, 134
Health Care Power of Attorney 122-127
Health Insight 100, 106
Health Insurance 2, 65-88, 143
Hearing 47, 59, 129, 133, 152, 154
Holographic will 110, 154
Home Health Care 69, 71, 74, 86, 89, 94-96
Hospice 69
Housing 89-106

I

Identity Theft 1, 5-8, 16-17, 21
Incapacitated 41, 131, 132, 154
Independent Living 97-98
Intestate 108-109
Investments 3

J

Joint Accounts 36, 107, 119
Joint tenancy 112, 118, 119, 154
Junk Mail 1, 9, 17

K

Kidney 66, 68
Kinship 39, 44-45, 48

L

Legal Help 145-152
Liability 12, 18, 96, 116
Lien 13
Life estate 118
Living Trusts 4
Living Will 121, 122, 125
Long Term Care 65, 148, 165
Long Term Care Insurance 65

M

Mediation 43, 48, 146, 151, 152, 154
Medicaid 6, 65, 82, 83, 85, 88, 94, 96, 117
Medicare 65-82, 84, 87, 88, 94, 95, 96, 100, 116
Medigap 82, 84, 88
Misdemeanor 37
Monitor 36, 132, 133

N

National Association of Home Builders 18
National Center for Assisted Living 88
National Committee for the Prevention of Elder Abuse 38
National Consumer Law Center 16
National Fraud Information Center 16
National Veterans Legal Services Program 64
Neglect 33-34, 37
Nursing Home 58, 60, 74, 83, 84, 89, 99-106

O

Office of Public Guardian 134
Ombudsman 100, 101, 103, 105, 106
Organ 124, 137, 144

P

Pension 49, 60-61, 62-64, 140, 141, 154
Pension Benefit Guaranty Corporation 62, 64
Pensions 49, 62
Personal representative 110, 111, 113, 115, 136, 139, 141
Pharmacy 80
Physical abuse 33, 37
Power of Attorney 35, 36, 121-127, 131-134, 154
Predatory Lending 3
Prescription 72, 73, 75, 83, 87
Probate 4, 107, 111-113, 114, 117, 119, 155

R

Railroad Retirement 68
Reconsideration 59, 78, 81, 82
Redetermination 81
Representative payee 58, 130, 153, 155
Retirement Communities 99
Reverse Mortgage 1, 13-15, 18
Revocation 122

S

Scams 1-5, 16
Self help resource center 146-148, 151
Senior Centers 93, 106
Senior Health Insurance Information Program 85, 87, 88

Senior Housing Net 106
Senior Residence 97-98
Skilled Nursing 69, 74, 84, 90, 95,
    100
Small Claims Court 21, 29, 147, 151
Social Security 5, 6, 26, 49-59, 61, 63,
    64, 68, 76, 130, 140, 142
Social Security Administration 6, 51,
    57, 59, 64, 130, 142
Social Security Disability Insurance
    54-55
State Inspection Reports 101

T
Taxes 116, 117, 118
Telemarketers 1, 9-10, 17
Terminating 25, 47
Toolkit 124, 134
TransUnion 16
Trust(ee) 4, 28, 63, 108, 112, 113-114,
    115, 130, 139

U
Unbundled legal services 149
Utah Attorney General 8, 17
Utah Department of Health 101, 106,
    127, 141, 144
Utah Department of Workforce
    Services 48
Utah Dispute Resolution 48
Utah Division of Aging and Adult
    Services 106, 134, 157
Utah Division of Child and Family
    Services 48
Utah Division of Consumer Protection
    5, 10, 16, 17, 18, 20, 21, 22, 29
Utah Division of Occupational and
    Professional Licensing 12, 18
Utah Division of Public Utilities 25,
    30
Utah Donor Registry 144
Utah Insurance Department 88
Utah Legal Services 30, 148, 152, 162
Utah Medicaid Program 88
Utah State Bar 120, 150, 151, 152, 162
Utah State Courts' Self-Help Resource
    Center 41, 46, 146, 147, 148,
    151
Utilities 24-25, 30

V
Verbal Contracts 19, 23
Veteran Benefits 49, 59-61, 64, 139
Visitation Rights 39, 42-44

W
Will 108-111

To order copies of the book, contact the Utah Division of Aging and Adult Services at 877-424-4640.

The primary author is willing to speak to groups on any topic presented in this book. Please contact Jilenne Gunther, Legal Enforcement Counsel, Utah Division of Aging and Adult Services at jgunther@utah.gov or 801-538-3910.